Harold Pinter was born in East London in 1930.
He is married to Antonia Fraser.

THE COMFORT OF STRANGERS
and other screenplays

REUNION

TURTLE DIARY

VICTORY

Harold Pinter

faber and faber

LONDON · BOSTON

First published in 1990
by Faber and Faber Limited
3 Queen Square London WC1N 3AU

Photoset by Wilmaset Birkenhead Wirral
Printed in Great Britain by
Richard Clay Ltd Bungay Suffolk

© Harold Pinter, 1990

Harold Pinter is hereby identified as author of this work in accordance with
Section 77 of the Copyright, Designs and Patents Act 1988.

The Comfort of Strangers is based on the novel *The Comfort of Strangers* by
Ian McEwan, published by Jonathan Cape Ltd; *Reunion* is based on the novel
Reunion by Fred Uhlman, published by Penguin Books Ltd; *Turtle Diary* is based
on the novel *Turtle Diary* by Russell Hoban, published by Random House Inc.;
Victory is based on the novel *Victory* by Joseph Conrad, published by Collins.

A CIP record for this book is available from the British Library
ISBN 0-571-14419-5
ISBN 0-571-14420-9 (PBK)

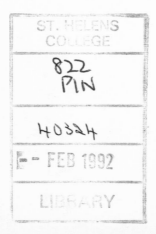

CONTENTS

The Comfort of Strangers

The Comfort of Strangers was made in 1990. The cast includes:

ROBERT	Christopher Walken
COLIN	Rupert Everett
MARY	Natasha Richardson
CAROLINE	Helen Mirren

Director of Photography	Dante Spinotti, AIC
Production Designer	Gianni Quaranta
Editor	Bill Pankow
Music	Angelo Badalamenti
Wardrobe	Giorgio Armani
Costume Supervisor	Mariolina Bono
Producer	Angelo Rizzoli
Director	Paul Schrader

INT. ROBERT'S APARTMENT: VENICE. EVENING

A long gallery. At the end of the gallery sliding glass doors give on to a terrace. Light from chandeliers is reflected in the glass.

Dark oil paintings. Dark mahogany cabinets, carved and polished, cushioned in velvet. Two grandfather clocks in a recess, ticking.

Stuffed birds and glass domes, vases, brass and cut-glass objects. A large polished dining-table.

The camera pans to a man's hand carefully setting a needle on to a record. The record starts. It is Gigli, singing an aria. The camera pans away, across a Nikon camera with a zoom lens and strips of developed film on a shelf.

The camera moves towards the glass doors. A painting: a landscape with leafless trees towering over a dark lake; on the shores shadowy figures dancing. A sideboard, a brass knob on every drawer in the shape of a woman's head.

On the top of the sideboard a tray of silver-backed men's hair and clothes brushes, a decorated china shaving bowl, several cut-throat razors arranged in a fan, a row of pipes in an ebony rack, a riding crop, a fly-swat, a gold tinder-box, a watch on a chain, a pair of opera glasses. Sporting prints on the wall.

The night sky through the glass doors. On the terrace an impression of flowering plants, creepers, trees in tubs, statuary.

Gigli's voice fades down.

ROBERT: (*Voice over*) My father was a very big man. All his life he wore a black moustache. When it turned grey he used a little brush to keep it black, such as ladies use for their eyes. Mascara.

Pause.

Everyone was afraid of him. My mother, my four sisters. At the dining-table you could not speak unless spoken to first by my father.

Pause.

But he loved me. I was his favourite.

CAROLINE *comes through a door into the gallery. She limps.*

3

She opens the glass doors and goes out on to the terrace. The camera reaches the glass doors and goes through on to the terrace, losing her. Sounds of concertinas and singing from below.

EXT. LAGOON. VENICE. DAY
A vaporetto passing.

EXT. WATERFRONT. DAY
Boats jiggling up and down in the wash of the vaporetto.

EXT. HOTEL ROOM: BALCONY. DAY
COLIN *standing on the balcony. He is leaning with one hand on the balcony wall, looking out on to the lagoon.*
MARY's *voice from inside the room.*
MARY: (*Voice over*) Yes, I want to call England –

A VIEWFINDER
COLIN's *figure framed in the viewfinder.*

BALCONY
COLIN's *arm and back leaning against wall. Lagoon in background.*
MARY: (*Voice over*) No, no, not London – it's not London.

CLOSE SHOT
Vaporetto.
A zoom lens moving.

EXT. HOTEL ROOM: BALCONY. DAY
COLIN *standing. Sound of a zoom lens.*
COLIN *turns, sits, picks up a loosely bound typescript, reads.*
The camera looks past him, through the open windows, to see MARY *holding the telephone.*
MARY: It's in Sussex. Hastings in Sussex . . . You know the
code, you got it for me yesterday . . . well, someone did
. . . yes – 458261 . . . Hastings, Sussex . . .
She puts the phone down.
God!
COLIN: I can't read this damn book! Honestly. It's unreadable.

Pages slip from his fingers on to the floor.
They can't even bind the bloody thing properly.
He slams the rest of the typescript on to the table.
Why don't we go out?

MARY: I'm trying to get through to the children! Can't you
hear?

The phone rings. MARY *picks it up.*
Hello? Yes? Mother! Hello! Yes – lovely – Yes, absolutely
– How are they? – Yes, lovely – are they? – Darling – it's
Mummy – How are you?

COLIN *closes his eyes.*

INT. CARPACCIO SCUOLA DI SAN GIORGIO
Dark interior. Carpaccio paintings. Silence. COLIN *and* MARY
stand looking at a painting (Visione de sant'Agostino).
*The camera moves through an arch to see them in long shot. Sound
of a scraping shoe on stone. The camera retreats.*

COLIN AND MARY WITH PAINTING
Scrape of shoe.
COLIN *looks over this shoulder.*
There is no one else in the chapel.
MARY: Incredible, isn't it?

EXT. SCUOLA. CANAL. DAY
They emerge into the light and walk.
MARY: I think the St Augustine is incredible, particularly, it's
     so . . . I don't know . . .
COLIN: Yes, you thought that last time.
MARY: What do you mean?
COLIN: Well, you said it was incredible last time – the last time
     we were in Venice.
MARY: Did I?
COLIN: Yes.
MARY: Well, so what?
COLIN: Nothing. I'm just—
MARY: I mean what's the *point*? What's the point of saying that?
     Why did you say that?

COLIN: (*Laughing*) I didn't mean it as an insult!

MARY: Christ.

COLIN: I'm simply making an observation –

MARY: What observation?

COLIN: I'm simply pointing out that you haven't changed your mind. You feel the same now as you did then.

FROZEN LONG SHOT: COLIN AND MARY BY SIDE OF CANAL

EXT. CANAL. DAY
He takes her hand.

COLIN: Anyway I agree with you. I think it's incredible too.

INT. HOTEL BATHROOM. DAY
COLIN *in the bathroom shaving. He cuts himself.*

COLIN: Shit!
    MARY *looks in.*

MARY: What is it?
    He dabs himself.

COLIN: Look. I think it was a pimple.

MARY: Tch. Tch. The girls won't love you any more.

COLIN: I think I need to eat more salt or something.

MARY: You don't need salt, you need sex.

COLIN: Can I have it with salt?

MARY: Why not?
    The phone rings.

COLIN: Oh, God! Don't they know I'm trying to shave?
    She picks up the phone.

MARY: Yes? Oh, hold on. (*Calls*) It's Simon.
    COLIN *sighs, goes into the room.* MARY *comes into the bathroom and begins to brush her hair.*
    COLIN *into phone.*

COLIN: Yes? . . . Oh, come on, give me a break – I'm only halfway through the damn thing – it's unreadable anyway – this is supposed to be my holiday – all right, all right, I'll finish it – when's the deadline?

INT. HOTEL BEDROOM. NIGHT
COLIN *and* MARY *in bed. She is asleep. His eyes are open. He looks at her, gets out of the bed, gets into the other bed and lies still.*

EXT. VENICE WATERFRONT. DAY
COLIN *and* MARY *at a stall, looking at T-shirts.* COLIN *selects two.*
COLIN: OK. This for Cathy. And this for Jack.
MARY: Lovely.
COLIN: What do you think?
MARY: They'll be thrilled.
    COLIN *pays for the T-shirts.*
COLIN: Now I'm going to do a little drawing of Cathy for Cathy
    . . . and a little drawing of Jack for Jack.
    He does two pencil drawings on the two bags.
    What do you think?
MARY: Fantastic. You're a genius.
    They walk away through tourists and pigeons. She stops,
    focuses her camera, takes a snap of COLIN.
    Smile.
    He smiles. She takes another snap. Two women stop and look
    at COLIN. MARY *turns to them, offering camera.*
    Would you take one of us?
WOMAN: (*Swedish*) Of course. Very much so.
    MARY *takes* COLIN's *arm. They stand.*
    The click of another camera offscreen. A man in a white suit
    passes.
    The WOMAN *takes the photograph.*

EXT. ROBERT'S TERRACE. NIGHT
Moonlight. The shrubs. Statuary.
Camera moves to find the back of CAROLINE's *head. A man's hand in a white-coated sleeve comes into the shot. It begins to massage her neck.*
ROBERT: (*Voice over*) My youngest sisters, Alice and Lisa, came
    to me in the garden and said, 'Robert, Robert, come to the
    kitchen quickly. Eva and Maria have a treat for you.'

EXT. VENICE SQUARE. NIGHT
The camera moves into the square. COLIN *and* MARY *voices over:*

MARY: Cathy's been selected for the football team, did I tell
you?

COLIN: What football team?

MARY: The school football team! What else?

COLIN: Oh.

MARY: Do you think it's dangerous – I mean to play with all
those boys? I mean – she's a girl.

COLIN: I know she is.

MARY: I think it's dangerous.

The camera finds COLIN *and* MARY *at a table with wine. Men
at another table look at them with interest, exchanging remarks
in low voices. It is not clear whether they are focusing on* MARY
or COLIN.

MARY: Tell me something. Tell me the truth. Do you like
children?

COLIN: What children?

MARY: My children.

COLIN: Yes. I like your children.

MARY: No. What I meant was, do you actually like children?

COLIN: You mean all children?

MARY: Children. Do you actually like children?

COLIN: You mean as such – you mean the species – as such?

MARY: What I mean is – the real truth is – you don't like
children.

COLIN: You mean you think I don't like *your* children?

MARY: What about me? Do you like me?

COLIN: I like you. Do you know why?

MARY: No. Why?

COLIN: I like you because you're always asking me such
challenging questions. You're always testing my intellect.
*She makes a lazy motion of slapping his face. He catches her
hand and kisses it.*

EXT. SECOND CAFE. S. GIACOMO DELL'ORIO. LATER

COLIN *and* MARY *at a table with wine.*

MARY: Did I ever tell you the terrible thing that happened to
me when I was a little girl, the worst thing that ever
happened to me?

COLIN: You never told me.

MARY: Well, I was about seven – or eight – and I was part of a gang of kids – boys and girls – and we were this gang . . .

COLIN: Uh-huh?

MARY: And one day some of them said, 'One member of this gang isn't really good enough to be a member of this gang and does everyone agree that we should throw that person out?' And I said, 'Yes! Yes!' I clapped –

COLIN: You clapped?

MARY: Yes. I clapped. And I said, 'Yes – throw this person out!' And you know who that person was?

COLIN stares at her.

COLIN: You.

MARY: Yes.

He stares at her.

COLIN: God. That's a terrible story.

INT. HOTEL LOBBY. NIGHT

The NIGHT PORTER lets COLIN and MARY in. They sway slightly.

COLIN: What do you say – up at dawn – Get into a speedboat. Where shall we go? (*To* PORTER) Where can we go?

PORTER: Murano. They blow beautiful glass. Very nice.

MARY: Murano. Lovely.

COLIN: (*To* NIGHT PORTER) What time's dawn?

PORTER: Dawn, signore?

COLIN: Daybreak! A speedboat at daybreak to go to Murano!

INT. ROBERT'S APARTMENT. KITCHEN. NIGHT

CAROLINE in the kitchen making tea. She fills the kettle with water and puts it on the stove and takes the lid off a jar of lime leaves.
There are two cups on a tray.
In the background, through the open kitchen door, a man in a white suit is sitting at a table.
Over this ROBERT's voice:

ROBERT: (*Voice over*) And on the table were two big bottles of lemonade, a cream cake, two packets of cooking chocolate and a big bunch of marshmallows. And Maria said, 'Look, darling, this is all for you.'

9

INT. MURANO. GLASS-BLOWING FACTORY
Glass being blown fiercely.

INT. MURANO. GLASS-BLOWING FACTORY
Glass exhibition in cabinets.
COLIN *and* MARY *perusing the objects.* COLIN *turns suddenly. He sees through glass the distorted figure of a man in a white suit.*
MARY: Look at this, this is beautiful.
> COLIN *turns to her, looks back through the glass. The figure has disappeared. He joins* MARY.
COLIN: What?

EXT. LAGOON. DAY
COLIN *and* MARY *in a speedboat, going fast. They are hanging on to the rails. The speedboat approaches the Grand Canal.*
Sound fades.
ROBERT: (*Voice over*) And Maria said, 'Look, darling, this is all for you.'

INT. HOTEL BEDROOM. NIGHT
COLIN *and* MARY *lying on their beds. He turns and looks at her.*
COLIN: Are you asleep?
> *No response.*
> *Colin gets off his bed, goes to her bed, stands looking down at her. She does not move. He goes to the window, opens the shutters.*
> *Cobalt light over the lagoon. He looks out. Gondolas jogging up and down.*
> *He goes to the bed and shakes her.*
> Mary. It's late. Mary.
> *She wakes up.*
MARY: What is it?
COLIN: We haven't had any dinner.
MARY: What's the time?
COLIN: Late.

INT. HOTEL LOBBY. NIGHT
COLIN *and* MARY *with* CONCIERGE.
CONCIERGE: No, no. Padovani will be closed.

COLIN: What about –

CONCIERGE: No, no. Is quite late. Too late. All closed. But I
know a very good bar. Late-night bar. Nice sandwich,
good drinks. Very nice place. Very easy to find.

COLIN: Fine. Can I take the map?

CONCIERGE: Is my only one. Sorry.

MARY: Let me look.

She peers at the map. The CONCIERGE *points to a section of
it.*

CONCIERGE: Here. You see? Very nice. You go straight out of
here. (*He makes a swivelling movement.*) And then you . . .
is right ahead. (*He points to map.*) Right there.

MARY: Uh-huh . . .

EXT. ACCADEMIA BRIDGE. A KIOSK. NIGHT

The kiosk is closed. COLIN *and* MARY *walk towards it.* COLIN
peers into it.

COLIN: Plenty of maps in there. Christ, you'd think a bloody
hotel porter would have more than one map!

EXT. A SQUARE. NIGHT

*A man stacking chairs outside a café. The square is empty. A dog
barking.*

EXT. A STREET. NIGHT

*Shop with television sets. Brightly lit window. On some of the TV
sets Italian housewives are stripping silently.*

They come to an alley.

COLIN: Down here.

MARY: How do you know?

They turn into the alley.

THE ALLEY

They walk down the alley towards another street.

COLIN: What do you think?

A STREET

A large furniture store. In the window an enormous bed. Two dummies lie on it on their backs, their arms up. One wears pyjamas, another a nightie. They are both smiling.

MARY: She reminds me of someone.

COLIN: Look at that headboard.

The headboard spans the width of the bed. Embedded in the upholstery are a telephone, a digital clock, light switches and dimmers, a cassette recorder and radio, a small refrigerated drinks cabinet.

It's like a Boeing 747. Listen – what do you think? Where are we? Is this right?

MARY: Yes. Definitely.

They walk on.

A wall filled with posters. Announcements, graffiti, etc. Mainly feminist.

Look at all this.

He peers.

COLIN: Gruppa Femminista di Venezia.

MARY: You know, women are really radical here. They're really aggressive. It's great.

COLIN: I wish we had a map.

MARY: They want convicted rapists castrated.

COLIN: You see that monument? I think we passed it about ten minutes ago.

MARY: Quite right too.

COLIN: What is?

MARY: To castrate rapists.

She walks on towards a long, dark, narrow alley.

COLIN: Where are you going?

MARY: This way.

He catches her up. The come to a water fountain. MARY *presses it. Water comes out.*

It works.

She drinks.

Tastes of fish.

They walk into the dark alley.

COLIN: I'm starving.

In the distance, in the dim light, a figure appears walking towards them, silently. It disappears into the shadows. COLIN *and* MARY *continue walking down the alley, their footsteps echoing.*

MARY: I think we're on the right track.

A MAN'S VOICE: So do I.

ROBERT *steps out of the dark into a pool of street light and stands blocking their path. He is thick-set, muscular. He wears a tight-fitting black shirt, unbuttoned almost to his waist. On a chain round his neck hands a gold imitation razor blade. He carries a camera over his shoulder. He laughs shortly.*

ROBERT: Good evening to you. You need help?

MARY: Well, we're looking for a place where we can get something to eat.

COLIN: Come on, Mary.

ROBERT: It's very late. There's absolutely nothing in that direction. But I can show you a very good place that way. *He grins and nods in the direction they have come from.*

COLIN: Look. We know there's a place down this way.

ROBERT: No, no. Closed. Everything is closed. My name is Robert. Trust me. I'll show you this place. You must both be terribly hungry. Come. It excites me to meet English people. I'm always eager to practise my English. I once spoke it perfectly. Such a beautiful language.

MARY *is examining posters on a wall. They join her and follow her gaze. She is looking at a crude stencil in red paint – a clenched fist within the female organ.* ROBERT *gestures to the wall.*

All these – are women who cannot find a man. They want to destroy everything that is good between men and women. They are very ugly. Now – would you like to eat some beautiful Venetian food?

MARY: I would absolutely love to.

COLIN *and* MARY *look at each other.*

COLIN: All right. Let's go.

VARIOUS SQUARES AND ALLEYS

The trio walking, ROBERT *leading the way. A man putting up shutters outside a shop calls to* ROBERT. ROBERT *laughs and waves. Two men standing in a dark doorway mutter something to* ROBERT *as they pass.* ROBERT *cackles. They finally reach a brightly lit doorway. A notice says* BAR.

INT. BAR

ROBERT *parts the strips of a plastic curtain for* MARY. *They all come down a steep flight of stairs into the bar, which is cramped and crowded. There are no women present. A few dozen young men, dressed mainly in black, sit on high stools at the bar or stand around listening to a song on the jukebox. The majority are smoking or craning a neck forward and pouting to have a cigarette lit or putting out a cigarette with swift jabs. The song on the jukebox is powerful and sentimental and comes to a triumphant climax. The men seem to be moved.*

COLIN *and* MARY *sit at a table.* ROBERT *comes from the bar carrying a bottle of wine, three glasses and some breadsticks in a jar. He sits.*

ROBERT: There is no food. I'm sorry. The cook is sick. It's a tragedy. I could kill him. I'm very sorry. But this is a wonderful wine. Full of nourishment.

He pours wine. They bite into the breadsticks.

Cheers.

COLIN *and* MARY: Cheers.

ROBERT: Now tell me – I am a man of immense curiosity – passionate curiosity. Are you married, you two?

COLIN: No.

ROBERT: But you live together? You live together in sin?

MARY: No.

ROBERT: Why not? In this day and age, no one would stop you. In this day and age, as you well know, there are no standards.

COLIN: What about you? Why don't you tell us about you?

He pours wine into his glass.

Who are you anyway?

ROBERT *stares at* MARY.

ROBERT: (*To* MARY) But you have a child? Am I right?

MARY: How did you know?

ROBERT: I feel it. (*He touches his heart.*) Here.

MARY: I have two children.

She takes photographs from her handbag.

14

A boy and a girl.

ROBERT *examines the photographs.*

ROBERT: This is your boy and your girl?

MARY: Yes.

ROBERT: Beautiful. Beautiful. (*To* COLIN) Not yours?

COLIN: Not mine.

ROBERT: Beautiful children. They take after their beautiful
    mother.

    MARY *giggles.*

MARY: Thanks.

    They all drink. She looks around the room.

    I like this place.

ROBERT: I am truly pleased.

MARY: Your English is terribly good.

ROBERT: I grew up in London. My wife is Canadian.

COLIN: Any more breadsticks?

    ROBERT *turns to the bar. He calls in Italian.*

ROBERT: More wine! More breadsticks!

MARY: Your wife is Canadian?

ROBERT: Oh, certainly.

MARY: How did you meet her?

ROBERT: Ah, that would be impossible to explain without
    describing my mother and sisters. And that would only
    make sense if I first described my father.

    *He pours from the second bottle. A song ends. Low
    conversations begin around the room.*

    ROBERT *stares into his glass. He suddenly looks old, lined. He
    murmurs.*

    In order to explain how I met my wife I would have to
    describe my father.

    He looks at them both intently.

    Do you want me to do that? Would you really like me to do
    that?

    They look at him.

    Shall I do that? What do you say?

COLIN: Why not?

    ROBERT *stares at* COLIN *and then speaks.*

ROBERT: My father was a very big man. All his life he wore a
    black moustache. When it turned grey he used a little

15

brush to keep it black, such as ladies use for their eyes.
Mascara.

During ROBERT's *speech, various images are seen from*
COLIN's *or* MARY's *point of view:*
a) Men combing their hair at the bar.
b) A woman, brought in by a man, sits alone at a table,
ignored.
c) Men's bodies pass close by their table on their way to the
urinal.
d) A man holding a chapstick at his lips.
e) A woman enters with a man, looks about, goes out, followed
by the man.
f) Glasses piling up on the bar, cigarettes piling up in ashtrays.
g) Rubbish being thrown into plastic bags and dragged out.
h) The bar emptying. Distant voices of men in the street.
ROBERT's *voice never stops. He chain-smokes throughout.*

Everybody was afraid of him. My mother, my four sisters.
At the dining-table you could not speak unless spoken to
first by my father.
But he loved me. I was his favourite.
He was a diplomat all his life. We spent years in London.
Knightsbridge.
Every morning he got out of bed at six o'clock and went to
the bathroom to shave. No one was allowed out of bed until
he had finished.
My eldest sisters were fourteen and fifteen. I was ten. One
weekend the house was empty for the whole afternoon.
My sisters whispered together. Their names were Eva and
Maria. Then they called me and they led me into my
parents' bedroom. They told me to sit on the bed and be
quiet. They went to my mother's dressing-table. They
painted their fingernails they put creams and powder on
their faces, they used lipstick, they pulled hairs from their
eyebrows and brushed mascara on their lashes.
They took off their white socks and put on my mother's
silk stockings and panties. They sauntered about the room,
looking over their shoulders into mirrors. They were

beautiful women. They laughed and kissed each other. They stroked each other. They giggled with each other. I was enchanted. They fed my enchantment.

It was a beautiful day. The sun began to set. They washed themselves, they put everything away, in its place, leaving no clue. They whispered to me that it was our secret, that we would keep it in our hearts for ever and never reveal it. MARY *puts her hand out to find* COLIN's *hand. He does not take it. Her hand remains on his knee.*

But that night at dinner I felt my father staring at me, staring deep into me. He chewed, swallowed. He put his knife and fork down, he looked at me. My heart started to beat, to thump, to beat, to thump. My father said, 'Tell me, Robert, what have you been doing this afternoon?' He knew. I knew he knew. He was God. He was testing me. And so I told him. I told him all that my sisters had done. I told him everything. My mother was silent. My sisters' faces were white. No one spoke. My father said, 'Thank you, Robert', and finished his dinner.

After dinner my sisters and I were called to my father's study. They were beaten with a leather belt, without mercy. I watched this.

COLIN *takes* MARY's *hand.*

A month later they took their revenge. We children were again alone in the house. My youngest sisters, Alice and Lisa, came to me in the garden and said, 'Robert, Robert, come to the kitchen quickly. Eva and Maria have a treat for you.' I was suspicious but I went. I was so innocent. On the kitchen table were two big bottles of lemonade, a cream cake, two packets of cooking chocolate and a big box of marshmallows. And Maria said, 'Look, darling, this is all for you.' 'Why?' I asked. 'We want you to be kinder to us in future,' she said. 'When you have eaten all this you will remember how nice we are to you – and then you will be nice to us.' This seemed reasonable. 'But first,' Eva said, 'you must drink some medicine. This is very rich food and this medicine will protect your stomach and help you to enjoy it.' I was too greedy to question this. I drank the medicine – only slightly disgusting – and then I ate the chocolate and the cake and the marshmallows and drank a bottle of lemonade. And they applauded and said that only a *man* could drink a second bottle of lemonade, it would be beyond my capabilities, and I said, 'Give it to me,' and I drank the second bottle and I finished the chocolates and the marshmallows and the cake and they said, 'Bravo, bravo!' And then the kitchen began to spin round me and I badly needed to go to the lavatory and then suddenly Eva and Maria held me down and tied my hands together with a long piece of rope behind my back and Alice and Lisa were jumping up and down singing, 'Bravo, Robert!' And Eva and Maria dragged me across the corridor and hallway and into my father's study. They took the key from the inside, slammed the door and locked it. 'Bye, bye, Robert,' they called through the keyhole. 'Now you are big Papa in his study.'

I was locked in my revered, my feared father's study, where he received the diplomatic corps of London, the élite of the world. And I puked and pissed and shat all over my father's carpets and walls.

MARY *clutches* COLIN's *hand*.

My father found me there. He said, 'Robert, have you been eating chocolate?' Then he nearly killed me. And then he didn't speak to me for six months.

I have never forgiven my sisters.

My only solace was my mother. I grew so thirsty . . . at night. She brought me a glass of water every night and laid her hand upon my brow. She was so tender. When my father was away I slept in her bed. She was so warm, so tender.

But one afternoon the wife of the Canadian Ambassador was invited to tea. She brought her daughter, Caroline. When my mother showed her mother our garden – we were left alone, the children. Suddenly Eva said, 'Miss Caroline, do you sleep with your mother?' Caroline said, 'No. Do you?' And Eva said, '*He* does.' And all my sisters giggled and Caroline looked at me and smiled and said, 'I think that's really awfully sweet.'

He smiles.

And she became my wife. Not at that moment of course.
We were both only eleven years old at the time.
He roars with laughter.

EXT. SOTTOPORTICO DELLA MALAVASIA. NIGHT
COLIN *and* MARY *wandering up a dark alley.*
COLIN: Where are we? Do you know?
MARY: God, I must sit down. I've got such a –
　　(*She clutches her head.*) Oh, I've got such a headache.
COLIN: What can I –
MARY: Press the back of my neck. That's right. Just there.
COLIN: There.
MARY: Yes.
COLIN: Is that . . . ?
　　They stand, COLIN *massaging her neck.*
MARY: I don't feel –
　　She lurches away, goes to the gutter, is sick.
　　COLIN *stands.*
　　She comes back.
　　I'm all right. Let's sit over there. I can't walk any more.
　　They sit on the steps of a dark house.
　　Hold me.
　　He does.
　　What a terrible man. (*She yawns.*) Who was he?
　　She closes her eyes.
　　He holds her.

EXT. SOTTOPORTICO. JUST BEFORE DAWN
COLIN *and* MARY *sitting.*
*She is leaning on him. He is leaning against the wall. They are
asleep.*
A Cellophane wrapper blows.
A dog passes by.
MARY *murmurs.*
MARY: We're on our holiday.

EXT. SOTTOPORTICO. DAYLIGHT
The two figures asleep against the wall. Children's voices, laughter.
A high-pitched bell.

They open their eyes.
Small children in bright-blue smocks approaching. COLIN *stands,*
holds his head. The children converge about him.
A little girl tosses a tennis ball against his stomach and catches it on
the bounce. Squeals of glee. The children pass on.

EXT. CAMPIELLO DE PIOVANO. MORNING
The street empty. MARY *is scratching her ankle.*
MARY: I've been bitten.
    COLIN *bends, looks, lifts her up.*
COLIN: Try not to scratch.
MARY: I'm so thirsty.
    She leans on his shoulder.
    You're going to have to look after *me* today.
COLIN: Did you look after me yesterday?
    He kisses her ear, holds her.
MARY: I'm so thirsty.
COLIN: I can see the waterfront. There'll be a café.
    They begin to walk towards the waterfront.

EXT. ST MARK'S SQUARE. MORNING
It is breakfast time. Hundreds of tourists are sitting at the café tables
eating.
COLIN *and* MARY *stand in the shade of an arch and look across the*
square. Every table seems to be taken.
They wander into the square and finally see an elderly couple at the
edge of a café writhing in their seats waving a bill. They stand by
the table. A waiter comes. The couple pay the bill and stand. COLIN
and MARY *sit down. The waiter clears the table.* COLIN *begins to*
speak. The waiter goes without taking an order.
COLIN *stands, goes to a group of waiters standing in the shade.*
COLIN: We're over there. We'd like something to drink.
WAITER: Yes, yes. I will tell your waiter.
    COLIN *walks back to the table and sits. At another table sits a*
    family. A baby stands on the table supported by its father,
    swaying among the ashtrays and empty cups. It wears a white
    sunhat, a green and white striped matelot vest, bulging pants
    frilled with white lace and pink ribbon, yellow ankle socks and

scarlet leather shoes. A dummy is in its mouth. its eyes are wild.
It is doing a mad dance.
COLIN *waves to a waiter, who passes by with a tray of empty*
bottles.
MARY *speaks through thick, dry lips.*
MARY: I wonder how the children are.
COLIN: You spoke to them – when was it?
MARY: Was it yesterday?
COLIN: How were they then?
    He waves to another waiter.
MARY: It's like a prison here.
    An orchestra starts to play, very close.
    Let's go home.
COLIN: Our flight is paid for and it doesn't leave for five days.
MARY: We could get a train.
COLIN: Why do you want to go home?
    COLIN *waves to a* WAITER. *The* WAITER *comes towards*
    him.
    I can't believe it! He's coming!
MARY: We should have brought the children with us. It would
    have made all the difference. To me anyway.
WAITER: Signore?
COLIN: A jug of water – with ice –
WAITER: *Water?*
COLIN: And coffee –
WAITER: Croissants? Eggs?
COLIN: No, no. Just a jug of water.
    The WAITER *turns and goes. They sit, slumped.*
MARY: Let's go to the hotel. Get water there.
COLIN: All right.
MARY: Oh, he's probably bringing the coffee anyway.
    They sit.
    I don't know why we came here. Why did we come? We've
    been here before. Why did we come again?
    He is silent.
    Actually, I remember why we came. We thought we'd find
    out what to do. Didn't we? What to do about you and me.
    Well . . . have you found out?
    He is silent.

21

I haven't. I just want to go home. To my own bed. And my
kids.
Pause.
Or maybe you have. Maybe you've decided what you want
– what you want to do.
Pause.
Have you?

COLIN: No.
*They suddenly tense. In their eyeline is a man in a white suit,
his back to them. A camera in his hand. He turns and walks in
their direction.*
We should have gone to the hotel.
ROBERT *walks along the edge of the tables.*
He's missed us.
ROBERT *turns, looks in their direction, opens his arms wide in
delight. He comes to the table.*

ROBERT: My friends!
He shakes COLIN'S *hand, kisses* MARY'S *hand. He sits.*
And how are you both this morning?

MARY: Terrible. We slept in the street.

ROBERT: The street?

MARY: After we left you. We were just too tired to . . .

COLIN: We didn't have a map –

ROBERT: I am horrified. It is entirely my fault. I kept you late
with wine, my stupid stories –

COLIN: (*To* MARY) Stop scratching. (*To* ROBERT) No, no, it's
not a question –

ROBERT: It is my fault and it is my responsibility to correct it.
You must come to my house –

COLIN: No – we have a hotel –

ROBERT: My house is a thousand times more comfortable,
peaceful, serene –
MARY *stands.*

COLIN: Wait a minute.
ROBERT *stands.*

ROBERT: We'll take a taxi.
ROBERT *takes* MARY'S *arm and walks with her across the
square.* COLIN *follows.*

EXT. ST MARK'S WATERFRONT. DAY
They walk through the crowds on to the waterfront. ROBERT *hails a taxi. They climb in.*

EXT. WATERFRONT BELOW ROBERT'S APARTMENT. DAY
The taxi arriving. ROBERT *helps* MARY *out.* COLIN *jumps off. They walk towards the house.*

INT. ROBERT'S APARTMENT. BEDROOM. DAY
The shutters half open. Light. COLIN *and* MARY *lie on two beds, naked, asleep.*
The click of a camera.
A soft sigh is heard, offscreen.
A door closes quietly.

INT. ROBERT'S APARTMENT. BEDROOM. LATE AFTERNOON
Through the half-open shutters, the setting sun. Orange bars against the wall. They fade, blur, brighten, fade.
MARY'S *eyes open. She watches this.* COLIN *remains asleep.*
Dry leaves rustle in the warm draught.
She stands, pours water from a jug, sips.
She looks down at COLIN, *gazes at his body.*
She goes to the window, opens shutters. Footsteps, sound of television, rattle of cutlery, dogs, voices. She closes the shutters, lies on the marble floor, starts to perform yoga exercises.
COLIN *suddenly wakes, sits up, looks at her on the floor.*
COLIN: Where are we?
MARY: Robert . . . brought us here.
COLIN: Robert. Where is he?
MARY: I don't know.
     He stands.
COLIN: What's the time?
MARY: Evening.
COLIN: Did you sleep?
MARY: Oh, yes. Wonderful.
COLIN: What about your bite?
MARY: It's gone.
     He looks around the room.
COLIN: Where are your clothes?

She looks at him.
Have you seen them? Where are they?
He walks to the bathroom, looks in, comes out.
They're not in there.
He opens a wardrobe. Looks in.
Nor in here.
MARY: No.
COLIN: Well, don't you think we ought to find them?
MARY: I feel good.
COLIN: I must find out what's going on. But I can't walk about
stark bloody naked.
MARY: Look. There's a dressing-gown on the back of that door.
COLIN: Oh, right.
He takes the gown and goes into the bathroom.
She lies still.
The toilet flushes.
(*Voice over*) I can't wear this!
*He comes out of the bathroom wearing the gown. She stares at
him.*
MARY: Oh yes you can. You look lovely. You look like a god. I
think I'll have to take you to bed.
She goes to him, feels his body beneath the gown.
COLIN: This isn't a dressing-gown. It's a nightie.
He points to an embroidered cluster of flowers.
MARY: You've no idea how good you feel in it.
He begins to take it off.
COLIN: I can't walk around in a stranger's house dressed like
this.
MARY: Not with an erection.
He gives the nightdress to her.
COLIN: Put it on. Find out what he's done with our clothes.
She slips it on, looks at herself in the mirror.
MARY: How do I look?

INT. ROBERT'S APARTMENT. GALLERY. EVENING
MARY *walking along the long gallery in the nightdress.*
*She looks through the glass door on to the terrace and sees a small
pale face watching her from the shadows, disembodied, oval. It
moves and disappears.*

The reflected room shakes as the glass doors open. A woman comes in.

CAROLINE: Hello. I'm Caroline. Robert's wife.

MARY: Hello.

They shake hands.

CAROLINE: Come outside. It's nice.

EXT. TERRACE. EVENING

Stars. The lagoon.

CAROLINE *lowers herself into a canvas chair. A little gasp of pain. She looks up at the sky.*

CAROLINE: It is beautiful. I spend as much time as possible out here.

MARY: I'm Mary . . . Kenway.

CAROLINE: Yes, I know.

MARY *sits. She fingers the sleeve of the nightdress.*

MARY: Is this yours?

CAROLINE: Yes. I made it. I sometimes sit out here doing embroidery. I like embroidery.

MARY: It's lovely.

MARY *looks at a plate of biscuits on a small table.*

CAROLINE: Would you like a biscuit? Take one.

MARY: Thanks.

CAROLINE: Are you hungry? You must be. Robert wants you to stay to dinner. He'll be back for dinner. He'd gone to his bar. A new manager starts there tonight.

MARY: His bar?

CAROLINE: You were there last night . . . weren't you?

MARY: He didn't say it was *his* bar.

CAROLINE: It's a kind of hobby, I guess. But you know more about it than I do. I've never been there.

She stands, moves awkwardly to the edge of the terrace.

MARY: Have you done something to your back?

CAROLINE: It helps to move. Sometimes I just stand up . . . and move about . . .

She stands looking over the edge of the terrace.

Are you fond of your friend?

MARY: Colin?

CAROLINE: I hope you don't mind. There's something I must tell you. While you were asleep I came in and looked at you both. I sat on the chest for about half an hour. I just sat there and looked at you . . . both.

MARY: Oh . . .

CAROLINE: Colin is very beautiful, isn't he? Robert said he was. You are too, of course. You both have such wonderful skin. Are you in love?

MARY: Well, I . . . I do love him, I suppose – but not quite like when we first met . . . But I trust him, really. He's my closest friend. But . . . what do you mean by 'in love'?

CAROLINE: I mean that you'd do absolutely anything for the other person . . . and you'd let them do absolutely anything to you.

MARY: Anything's a big word.

CAROLINE: If you're in love with somebody, you'd be prepared –

The glass doors open. COLIN *comes out on to the terrace, a towel around his waist.*

MARY: This is Colin. This is Caroline, Robert's wife.

CAROLINE: Hello. Are you having a nice time?

COLIN: Uuhh . . .

CAROLINE: On your holiday?

COLIN: Oh . . . yes . . . except we keep getting lost.

CAROLINE: Pull up a chair.

COLIN *draws a canvas chair nearer to them and sits, carefully adjusting his towel.*

Oh my God! Your clothes! (*She laughs.*) I forgot! I washed and dried them. I clean forgot. I must tell you where they are. (*She turns to* MARY.) But before I do I think you should tell him what I told you . . . don't you?

MARY: What?

CAROLINE: What I did while you were both asleep.

MARY: Oh. (*To* COLIN) Caroline came in and looked at us while we were asleep.

COLIN: Oh . . . did she?

CAROLINE: (*To* COLIN) You were so peaceful. Like a baby.

MARY: Babies can be very ratty in their sleep.

CAROLINE: But not him. I'm sure he always sleeps sweetly.

COLIN: But I'm not a baby.

CAROLINE laughs.

CAROLINE: I didn't say you were. I just said you slept like a baby. Now listen, Robert is very keen for you to stop and have dinner with us. He told me not to let you have your clothes until you agreed. (*She giggles.*) You must be starving anyway.

COLIN: I am.

CAROLINE: So you will?

MARY: Well . . .

CAROLINE grasps her arm.

CAROLINE: Please! If you don't he'll blame me.

COLIN: Let's stay.

CAROLINE: Oh good!

COLIN: And now can I have my clothes?

CAROLINE giggles.

CAROLINE: They're locked in your bathroom cupboard. Here's the key.

He takes it, holding his towel to him.

COLIN: I'll just . . .

He goes into the gallery. CAROLINE *looks after him. She turns to* MARY.

CAROLINE: Isn't it sweet, when men are shy? It's so sweet.

She smiles at MARY.

Tell me what you do. Do you work?

MARY: Well, I mainly do voice-overs these days, you know . . . commercials. I *was* with a women's group until about six months ago –

CAROLINE: What do you mean? What do you mean by a women's group?

MARY: A theatre group.

CAROLINE: You're an actress! What a beautiful thing that must be.

MARY laughs.

MARY: Well, sometimes . . . Anyway, the group broke up –

CAROLINE: Women? All women?

MARY: Well, some of us wanted to bring in men – from time to

27

time. The others wanted to keep it pure. That's what broke us up.

CAROLINE: But how can you do a play with only women? I mean what could *happen*?

MARY: Happen? (*She laughs.*) Well, you could have a play about two women who've only just met sitting on a balcony talking.

CAROLINE: But they'd probably be waiting for a man. And then he'd come. And then something would happen.

CAROLINE giggles. She clasps her back.

It hurts when I laugh.

MARY: Can I do . . .

CAROLINE: Yes. Touch me there. My neck.

MARY does so.

Press it. A little harder.

MARY does so and then stops.

Thank you.

MARY: (*Uneasily*) We did an all-woman *Hamlet* once.

CAROLINE: *Hamlet*? I've never read it. I haven't seen a play since I was at school. Isn't it the one with the ghost?

Lights go on in the gallery behind them. Footsteps.

And someone locked up in a convent?

Footsteps stop, start. A chair scrapes. Sound of glass.

ROBERT comes out on to the terrace.

ROBERT: Hello!

CAROLINE limps across the terrace into the apartment. ROBERT does not look at her. He crosses to MARY, smiling. He is wearing black.

Have you slept well?

MARY: Wonderfully. Thank you so much. What a beautiful apartment.

ROBERT: It belonged to my grandfather.

He takes MARY's elbow and leads her to the edge of the terrace. He points across the lagoon.

You see that island? That is Cemetery Island. My grandfather and my father are both buried there. You're staying for dinner, I trust?

MARY: I'll get dressed.

He leads her into the apartment.

INT. THE GALLERY

ROBERT: A glass of champagne first!

A bottle and four glasses are set on the table.

ROBERT *opens the bottle.* COLIN *comes into the gallery, dressed and shampooed. His shirt and jeans have been cleaned and ironed. They cling to his body.* ROBERT *stares at him as he walks slowly towards them.*

You look like an angel. (*Calls*) Caroline! (*To* COLIN) How are you feeling?

COLIN: Better.

ROBERT *pours the champagne.* CAROLINE *appears. She takes her place at* ROBERT'*s side facing the guests. They lift their glasses.*

CAROLINE: To Colin and Mary.

They drink. MARY *laughs shortly. She drinks.* CAROLINE *turns and goes into the kitchen.*

MARY: I'll dress.

She goes. COLIN *drinks.* ROBERT *fills his glass. He takes* COLIN'*s elbow and steers him gently down the gallery to a carved mahogany bookcase.*

ROBERT: You see these books? They are the favourite literature of my father and my grandfather. All first editions.

He steers COLIN *to a sideboard. On top of the sideboard, hairbrushes, clothes brushes, pipes, razors, etc., a pair of opera glasses.*

These are things my father used every day. Small things.

They look at them in silence.

COLIN: He used opera glasses every day?

ROBERT *stares at him.*

ROBERT: No. He used opera glasses at the opera. They belonged to my grandfather.

They move to the champagne. ROBERT *empties the bottle.*

COLIN: Your father is very important to you.

ROBERT: My father and his father understood themselves clearly. They were men and they were proud of their sex. Women understood them too. Now women treat men like children, because they can't take them seriously. But men like my father and my grandfather women took very seriously. There was no uncertainty, no confusion.

29

COLIN: So this is a museum dedicated to the good old days.

COLIN bends to put his glass down. As he straightens ROBERT *hits him in the stomach with his fist, a relaxed, easy blow which sends* COLIN *jack-knifing to the floor. He lies on the floor writhing, fighting for air.* ROBERT *takes the empty glasses to the tray. He comes back, helps* COLIN *to his feet, makes him bend at the waist and straighten several times.* COLIN *breaks away, walks about the room, taking deep breaths, dabbing his eyes.*

ROBERT *lights a cigarette and walks to the kitchen door. He turns and looks back.* COLIN *glares blearily at him.*

ROBERT *winks.*

INT. APARTMENT. NIGHT

The dinner table. ROBERT *in a pale-cream suit.* MARY *in her clean dress.* CAROLINE *in another dress. They are eating steak and drinking red wine.* COLIN *sits slightly removed from the others, eating slowly.*

ROBERT: So how is England? Lovely dear old England? Hampshire! Wiltshire! Cumberland! Yorkshire! Harrods! Such a beautiful country. Such beautiful traditions.

MARY: It's not quite so beautiful now. Is it, Colin?

COLIN *does not respond.*

Colin? Are you feeling all right?

COLIN: (*Quietly*) Sure.

ROBERT: In what way? In what way not beautiful?

MARY: Oh, I don't know – freedom . . . you know . . .

ROBERT: Freedom? What kind of freedom? Freedom to do what?

MARY: Freedom to be free!

ROBERT: You want to be free? (*He laughs.*) Free to do what?

MARY: You don't believe in it?

ROBERT: Sure I believe in it. But sometimes a few rules – you know – they're not a bad thing. First and foremost society has to be protected from perverts. Everybody knows that. My philosophical position is simple – put them all up against a wall and shoot them. What society needs to do is purify itself. The English government is going in the right direction. In Italy we could learn a lot of lessons from the English government.

COLIN: Well, I'm an Englishman and I disagree violently with what you've just said. I think it's shit!

ROBERT: I respect you as an Englishman, but not if you're a communist poof. You're not a poof, are you? That's the right word, no? Or is it 'fruit'? Talking about fruit – it's time for coffee.

They all stand.

COLIN: We must go.

CAROLINE: But coffee –

COLIN: No. We must go. Now.

MARY: Yes, it's been a long day.

MARY *suddenly sees a bookcase upon which a number of photographs stand. She walks to it and peers.* ROBERT *joins her.*

ROBERT: I'm a keen amateur photographer.

MARY *focuses on a large photograph, which is grainy and indistinct. It is taken from some distance and seems to have been enlarged many times. It is of a man standing on a balcony of a hotel, leaning with one hand on the wall.*

She picks it up and looks at it. ROBERT *looks at her looking at it for a few seconds and then takes it from her.*

CAROLINE *whispers to* COLIN.

CAROLINE: Please come back. Please. It's important. I can't get out.

COLIN: Come on, Mary.

She turns from the bookcase.

MARY: Well, thank you both so much for your hospitality – and for such a lovely dinner.

ROBERT: It has meant a great deal to us.

EXT. STREET. NIGHT

COLIN *and* MARY *walking hand in hand.*

INT. HOTEL ROOM. BALCONY. NIGHT

COLIN *and* MARY *sitting in the moonlight.*

COLIN: You know – when I came on to the balcony tonight and

saw you in that nightdress – I thought you looked so
beautiful, my heart . . . jumped.

MARY: But I told you how *you* looked in that nightdress, didn't
I?

*They sit in silence. After a while, they stand and go into the
room.*

A heavy green curtain is drawn across the window.

Moon on the balcony. A moan from within the room.

EXT. HOTEL ROOM. BALCONY WINDOW. DAY

Shutters closed.

Sun striking the shutters.

A long sigh from within the room.

COLIN: (*Voice over*) Jesus!

INT. HOTEL BEDROOM. DAY/NIGHT

The room is suffused with green light, neither night nor day.

A knock on the door.

A maid peeps in.

MAID: Permesso?

COLIN: (*Voice over*) Please!

MAID: We must clean the room.

COLIN: (*Voice over*) We're on our bloody holiday, for Christ's
sake!

The maid withdraws.

MARY: (*Voice over, whispering*) Come here, come here.

INT. HOTEL BEDROOM. DAY/NIGHT

*The mattress has been taken from one of the beds, propped against
the door.*

Clothes and glasses on the floor.

COLIN *and* MARY *lie partially clothed half on, half off the bent
mattress.*

COLIN: What's it like? I often wonder what it's like.

MARY: What's what like?

COLIN: To be a girl. How does it feel? What does it feel like?

MARY *looks at him and smiles.*

MARY: Like this.

She places her tongue in his ear and moves it about.

INT. HOTEL CORRIDOR. DAY/NIGHT
Food stacked on trolley outside the room, half eaten.

INT. HOTEL BEDROOM. NIGHT
COLIN *and* MARY *asleep, lying across each other on the bed. Green glow.*
MARY (*Voice over, softly*) I'm crazy about you.
>*Their eyes suddenly open. They turn, twist, look at each other. They kiss.*
COLIN: I'm crazy about you.

INT. HOTEL CORRIDOR. DAY/NIGHT
Sheets and towels stacked alongside the trolley.

INT. HOTEL BEDROOM. DAY/NIGHT
MARY, *naked, looking through the green curtains on to the lagoon.*
COLIN *seen dimly in background in the room. He lies on the bed.*
COLIN: Close the shutters.
>*She closes them.*
>Come here.
>*She goes to him.*

EXT. LA COLOMBA RESTAURANT. NIGHT
COLIN *and* MARY *eating pasta.*
COLIN: Listen. Why the hell did they do that to you? Those kids. Why did they hound you out of the gang? I can't understand it.
MARY: They didn't like me.
COLIN: They were just jealous of you. That's what it was. They were jealous of your beauty.
>*He takes her hand. She giggles.*
>I am myself. You know that, don't you? I'm jealous of your beauty. I mean it belongs to me. Jealous in that sense. No one else can touch your beauty. It's all mine.
MARY: Is it?
COLIN: All mine.
>*He nuzzles her hand.*
>*Well-dressed Venetians are at another table. One woman,*

sumptuous, vivid, bejewelled, eyes COLIN *and* MARY, *murmurs
to the others.*
*The others look across, smile. The woman speaks in a low
voice. Another woman laughs.*

MARY: You know what they're doing?

COLIN: No, what?

MARY: They're talking about us.

COLIN: About you.

MARY: No. You.

COLIN: Or perhaps us?

    They laugh.

    Hey, listen, this actually reminds me – I wanted to ask
you –

MARY: What?

COLIN: Well, you know all this thing about thighs and bottoms?

MARY: What thing?

COLIN: Well – you know – people look at other people's thighs
and bottoms and they say, 'Christ, what thighs, what
bottoms – or what an arse – or an ass, what an *ass* – or tits
of course – what . . . tits . . . or what boobs . . . or what a
can,' if you see what I mean. I mean – what I mean is – I
mean my first point is – that only the word thighs is
constant. Get me? You've got all these other words for all
the other words. But there's no other word for thighs. Isn't
it amazing?

MARY: You don't need another word. Thighs is a perfectly good
word. What's your question?

COLIN: I'm really very glad that you've asked me what my
question is. It's this. When people look at you and . . . you
know . . . talk about your thighs or your bottom or both,
etc. . . . well, are you sensing them in the same way that
they're sensing them? I mean, to what extent are you
sensing their sense of you – or when I say you – I mean
your thighs and your bottom – in other words – listen – to
put it in a nutshell – when people talk about your thighs
and bottom – what sense of your thighs and your bottom
do you, at such a time, have?

MARY: People are not talking about my thighs and bottom.

COLIN: How can you – how can you *know* that?

MARY: Because the whole damn restaurant is talking about your thighs and bottom.

COLIN: Mine? I don't believe it.

He looks round at the other tables.

Really?

The woman at the other table catches his eye. COLIN *turns back to* MARY.

Incredible.

They giggle.

INT. HOTEL BEDROOM. NIGHT

MARY *at dressing-table putting cream on her face.*

COLIN *stretched out in an armchair reading a newspaper.*

MARY: (*Casually*) Oh, I forgot to tell you . . .

COLIN: (*Vaguely*) What?

MARY: I had rather a good idea . . .

COLIN: Uh-huh?

MARY: Mmnn. I'm going to hire a surgeon – a very handsome surgeon – to cut off your arms and your legs –

COLIN: Oh yes?

MARY: Yes. And then you'll be quite helpless, you see. I'll keep you in a room in my house . . . and use you just for sex, whenever I feel like it.

COLIN: Uh-huh . . .

MARY: That's right. And sometimes I'll lend you to my girlfriends . . . and they can do what they like with you . . .

COLIN: Oh, right.

MARY *stands, slips into bed, picks up a book, starts to read.* COLIN *continues to read the newspaper. Silence.*

It's funny you should say that . . . because I've sort of come to a decision . . . and I haven't told you yet . . .

MARY: A decision?

COLIN: Yes, I've come to this decision . . .

MARY: (*Turning a page*) What is it?

COLIN: Well, it's this – I'm going to invent a machine . . . you see . . . made of steel. It's powered by electricity. It has pistons and controls –

MARY: Oh, really?

COLIN: That's right. It has straps and dials. It makes a low hum
. . . like this . . .
He hums.

MARY: Like that?

COLIN: Yes. And you'll be strapped in . . . you see . . . quite
securely . . . tight . . . and the machine will fuck you – not
just for hours and weeks but for years and years and years.
For ever.

MARY: For ever?

COLIN: That's right.
He walks over to the bed, sits on it.
What do you think?

INT. HOTEL BEDROOM. DAWN
COLIN *and* MARY *are asleep.*
MARY *suddenly gasps and shouts out and sits up. She clasps her
knees, trembling.*
COLIN *wakes. He holds her. She recoils from his touch.*

COLIN: You're having a nightmare.
He touches her again. She wrenches free, gets out of bed.
A door opens. Footsteps in the corridor.
She stands still. COLIN *gets out of bed.*
Mary?
*She looks at the bed, walks to the window. Goes out. He
follows.*

EXT. HOTEL BALCONY. DAWN
COLIN: What was it? You've had a terrible dream. What –
She puts her finger to her lips.
She indicates to COLIN *that he stand in a precise position on
the balcony. She turns him to face out to the lagoon, lifts his
hand so that it rests on the balcony wall. She studies him.*

MARY: You're beautiful.

COLIN: Are you awake?
She stumbles into his arms, kissing him wildly.

MARY: I'm so frightened.
She begins to shake violently.

COLIN: What is it? What is it?

MARY: Touch me.
He pulls her back inside the room.

INT. HOTEL BEDROOM. DAWN
He sits her down on the bed and holds her shoulders hard.
COLIN: Are you awake? Mary?
She gradually becomes still.
You had a nightmare. Do you remember it?
She lies back on the bed. He lies by her, takes her hand. He yawns.
Can you tell me?
MARY: That photograph on Robert's bookcase was of you.
COLIN: What photograph?
MARY: I looked at a photograph in Robert's apartment. It was on his bookcase. It was of you.
COLIN: Of me?
MARY: It must have been taken from out there – along the waterfront – or from a boat . . . You were standing on this balcony.
COLIN: I didn't see any photograph –
MARY: No, you didn't see it.
They lie still.
Don't fall asleep. Keep awake.
COLIN: I'm awake.
MARY *whimpers.*
MARY: You're in his photograph.
Silence.
Colin?
He is still, breathing quietly.
She suddenly leans over him and looks down at him.
She kisses him.

EXT. LIDO BEACH. DAY
Large crowds on the beach.
Solitary men and women, bodies oiled.
Transistors.
Babies.
Babble of children playing.
COLIN *and* MARY *walking through this, looking for a place to rest.*

They settle finally near two teenage girls. A small knot of young men close by are turning cartwheels, etc.

COLIN *and* MARY *sit.*

MARY: Turn on your front.

He lies on his stomach. She sits astride him, rubs oil on his back.

The young men start to throw a ball hard at each other. The ball hits one of the girls. She cries out. All the young men immediately drop to their haunches and introduce themselves to the girls.

COLIN: (*Murmuring*) Something happened at Robert's flat. I didn't tell you.

MARY: I can't hear you. What?

COLIN: Something happened at Robert's flat. I didn't tell you. When you had gone to change – to dress – remember? – He was talking to me . . . about his father and so on and then he suddenly hit me in the stomach – very hard. He . . . totally winded me.

MARY: He hit you?

COLIN: Yes.

MARY: But why?

Pause.

You didn't say anything – why didn't you say anything?

COLIN: I don't know. I don't know why he hit me. And I don't know why I didn't say anything. And I don't know why he took a photograph of me on the hotel balcony either.

She rolls off his back and lies still. She stands.

MARY: I'm going to swim.

She walks towards the water.

EXT. LIDO BEACH. AFTERNOON

COLIN *and* MARY *walking along the beach. A beach vendor approaches.*

COLIN: I want to buy you something.

She smiles.

MARY: Why?

COLIN: Choose something.

MARY: No, you. You choose.

He looks at a selection of scarves, selects one.

COLIN: This.
MARY: Lovely.
COLIN: Try it.
  She puts it round her neck.
MARY: OK?
COLIN: Lovely.
  The sun goes behind a cloud.

INT. ROBERT'S APARTMENT. DAY
The glass doors on to the balcony. Silence.
The sun comes out.
The Gigli record begins.

EXT. LIDO BEACH. AFTERNOON
COLIN *and* MARY *walking along the water's edge. The beach is
emptying. The sun is low over the water. She stops and looks out to
sea. He touches her arm.*
COLIN: Listen. I've been thinking –
  She looks at him.
  Why don't we do it?
MARY: Do what?
COLIN: Get together. Live together . . . you know . . . with the
  children . . .
  She stands, looking at him.
  I mean it. I love you.
  She looks at him.
  I love you.
  She smiles.
  I mean it.
MARY: Yes, but . . . we don't have to . . . commit ourselves to
  all that . . . just now. I mean . . . it's such a lovely day.
COLIN: Don't you want to? I thought you wanted to.
MARY: I've just had such a wonderful swim, that's all. It was so
  beautiful – I can't describe it. I could have gone on for
  ever. I can't get back to . . . things like this . . . just like
  that.
  COLIN *laughs.*
COLIN: Things like this?
MARY: I was so happy swimming.

39

Pause.
COLIN: I thought you wanted it.
MARY: Oh, we'll see. Shall we?

INT. ROBERT'S APARTMENT. DAY
The gallery. Gigli singing. ROBERT's *hand picks up an object from the windowsill. He draws the blinds.*
Sun glinting through the chinks.
MARY: (*Voice over*) It goes round the other side of the island
    first.

EXT. QUAYSIDE/LIDO/VAPORETTO OFFICE
The vaporetto is approaching. COLIN *and* MARY *are studying the schedule in the ticket office.*
MARY: It goes round the other side of the island first. Then it
    cuts through by the harbour round to our side.

INT. ROBERT'S APARTMENT. BEDROOM
Hands folding a white suit on a bed. An empty suitcase.
Gigli.

EXT. VAPORETTO/GIARDINI. DAY
COLIN *and* MARY *sitting on adjacent benches, not speaking.*
The vaporetto slows to its landing by the hospital. Groups of old people waiting. The boat stops, the old people get on. The boat moves off.
In background, Gigli singing, faintly.

INT. ROBERT'S APARTMENT
Hands wrapping a riding crop, a fly swat, a watch on a chain, a pair of opera glasses.
COLIN: (*Voice over*) We could get off at the next stop and walk
    through if you like . . .

EXT. VAPORETTO MOVING
MARY *turns to him.*
MARY: What?
COLIN: We could get off at the next stop and walk through if

you like. It's probably quicker than going right round the
harbour.

MARY: Possibly . . . yes.

The vaporetto approaches the landing.

She kisses him lightly on the lips.

The vaporetto stops, the barrier is lifted. COLIN *and* MARY
stand quickly, walk off the boat on to the landing stage.

The pilot calls sharply to the crew, who lift the rope clear.

From inside the boat sudden laughter.

Gigli singing faintly.

EXT. QUAYSIDE. DAY

*Rope being drawn back on to the ferry. The ferry draws away from
the quayside.*

COLIN *and* MARY *walk in silence along the quayside. Gigli is
singing faintly.*

They look up.

On a balcony hung with flowers, a small figure in white waving.

Soft throb of the departing vaporetto.

CAROLINE'S *distant voice calling.*

MARY *stops.*

MARY: Do you want to go up there?

COLIN: Well, she's seen us. We can't be rude.

*They hail a gondola. They do not hold hands or look at each
other.*

INT. APARTMENT HOUSE. STAIRWELL

COLIN *and* MARY *come into the stairwell. She hesitates. He goes up
a few steps, turns, looks down at her. He leans against the wall – as
in the photograph. She stares at him.* ROBERT *appears looking down
from a top landing.*

ROBERT: Hello!

COLIN: Hello.

They walk up. CAROLINE *is standing in the doorway of the
apartment.* ROBERT *descends.*

ROBERT: How delightful. How delightful to see you.

He claps COLIN *on the back. Kisses* MARY'S *cheek.*

MARY: The boat brought us round this side from the beach, so
we thought we'd say hello.

41

ROBERT: We were expecting you sooner.
> *They reach the door.* CAROLINE *offers her cheek to* COLIN *and to* MARY.

CAROLINE: How lovely.

ROBERT: You got my message?

COLIN: No. What?

ROBERT: I left a message at your hotel today. We're going away, you see. We didn't want to miss you.

COLIN: No, we didn't get it.

ROBERT: But you came anyway! How wonderful.

MARY: Going away?

CAROLINE: To Canada. To see my family. So we wanted to say goodbye, to have a farewell drink – so it's wonderful you came. It really is.

ROBERT: (*To* CAROLINE) Look, take Mary and give her some refreshment. (*To* COLIN) I have to go to my bar. I have business to finish. Very quick. Will you come with me?
> CAROLINE *draws* MARY *in through the door.*

CAROLINE: Have you been swimming?

COLIN: (*To* MARY) I'll just –

ROBERT: Walk with me. Keep me company. (*To* MARY) We won't be long.

MARY: Colin –
> ROBERT *closes the door.*

INT. APARTMENT

MARY *looks about her. The apartment is transformed. Furniture, pictures, rugs, etc., have all gone. There is a makeshift table sitting on three boxes. A number of suitcases stand by the door. Her sandals echo loudly.*

MARY: Good God. I thought you were just going on a holiday. Are you moving?

CAROLINE: We're selling up. We *are* taking a holiday but when we come back we'll buy a ground-floor apartment. That's what I need. Would you like some herb tea?

EXT. STREET. DAY

ROBERT *and* COLIN *walking.* ROBERT *waves to some men outside a bar, looks at* COLIN.

INT. APARTMENT. KITCHEN
CAROLINE *reaches for the kettle. She winces.*
MARY: Can I do anything?
CAROLINE: It's been like this a long time now.
 She puts the kettle on the gas stove, turns on the gas.

EXT. VENICE SQUARE
ROBERT *stops at a café. He is holding* COLIN's *elbow. He speaks to some men. They laugh.*
A hand pinches COLIN's *buttock. He turns.* ROBERT *pulls him on. Laughter follows them.*
COLIN: Someone just pinched me.
ROBERT: Venetians are very friendly people.

INT. APARTMENT. KITCHEN
CAROLINE *pouring tea into two cups. She stirs.*
CAROLINE: Robert said he told you about his childhood. He
 exaggerates a lot, you know. He turns his past into stories
 to tell at the bar.
MARY: No sugar for me.
CAROLINE: Just stirring in the lemon to make it taste. Shall we
 take it on to the terrace?
 They move to the door.
MARY: What happened to your back?

INT. ROBERT'S BAR
ROBERT *behind the bar examining documents with the manager.*
COLIN *sitting with a mineral water at a table.* ROBERT *glances at him.*
One customer and then another glance at COLIN.
COLIN *prises open pistachio nuts, sips his drink, tilts the chair back.*
The bar very quiet. ROBERT *murmuring to the manager.*
COLIN *goes to the jukebox, looks at the lights, puts a coin in.*

EXT. TERRACE. EARLY EVENING
CAROLINE *and* MARY *sitting sipping tea.*
CAROLINE: I've never told anyone this. Never.
 But I want to tell you.
 Soon after we were married Robert started to hurt me when

we made love. Not a lot, enough to make me cry out. I tried
to stop him but he went on doing it. After a time I found I
liked it. Not the pain itself – but somehow – the fact of being
helpless before it, of being reduced to nothing by it – and
also being punished, therefore being guilty. I felt it was right
that I should be punished. And I thrilled to it.
It took us over totally. It grew and grew. It seemed never-
ending.
But there was an end to it. We both knew what it was. We
knew what it had to be. We knew it. We wanted it.

INT. BAR
Music from the jukebox bursts out.
ROBERT *comes and sits with* COLIN *with his documents.*
ROBERT: Did you understand what I was telling people as we
walked here?
COLIN: No.
ROBERT: I was telling them you are my lover. And that Caroline
is jealous because she likes you too.
The music stops.
COLIN: Why? Why were you telling them that?
ROBERT *laughs and mimics* COLIN.
ROBERT: Why? Why?
He touches COLIN's *hand.*
We knew you would come back.
COLIN: Why did you take the photo of me – the one you
showed Mary?
ROBERT: Aah. She's very quick. I thought I hadn't given her
enough time . . . to recognize it.
COLIN: What was the point?
A man turns the jukebox on. ROBERT *winks at* COLIN *and
indicates the manager at the bar.*
ROBERT: I'm selling the bar – to him.
He smiles.

EXT. TERRACE
CAROLINE *and* MARY *sitting.*
CAROLINE: My back happened – suddenly – one night. It was
very bad indeed. Then there was an incompetent surgeon

44

. . . you know. So I'm like this. I've never told anyone the truth – except you.

She takes MARY's *hand.*

He's terribly strong, you see. When he pulled my head backwards I blacked out with the pain – but I remember thinking: It's going to happen now. I can't go back on it now. It's going to happen – now. This is it. This is the end.

MARY *yawns.*

I'm boring you.

MARY: No, not at all. It's the long swim, I think, the sun . . .

CAROLINE: Do you and Colin do . . . strange things?

MARY: Oh, no. I don't think so.

CAROLINE: I'm sure Colin does. I'm certain he does.

She stands.

There's something I want to show you.

MARY *stands, sways, nearly falls.*

MARY: Oops.

CAROLINE *holds her.*

Bit dizzy.

CAROLINE: I must show you something.

EXT. FONDAMENTA NOVA. EVENING

ROBERT *and* COLIN *walking.*

ROBERT: You see that barber shop? My grandfather and my father used that barber shop. And I use that barber shop.

ROBERT *waves to a waiter standing outside a café.*

COLIN: I want to know why you took that photo? What does it mean?

ROBERT: That waiter was once a fisherman. But pollution has ruined the fish. So fishermen become waiters. (*Points.*) That is Cemetery Island.

COLIN *stops.*

ROBERT *walks on.*

COLIN *turns, looks out to the Cemetery Island and then down a long side street, light at the end.*

ROBERT *stops, half turns, stands still, waiting.*

45

INT. APARTMENT. BEDROOM
The bedroom is in semi-darkness. CAROLINE *and* MARY *enter.*
CAROLINE: You haven't been in our bedroom, have you?
   MARY *sits heavily on the edge of the bed.*
MARY: My legs ache.
   CAROLINE *turns on a lamp.*
   MARY *suddenly sees the wall. She stares at a wide baize-covered board, upon which are dozens of photographs of* COLIN.
   CAROLINE *sits with her.*
CAROLINE: God, he's so beautiful. Robert saw you both by
   chance, the day you first arrived.
   She points to a photograph of COLIN *standing by a suitcase, street map in hand, talking.*
   CAROLINE *holds* MARY.
   That was the first picture I saw of him. I'll never forget it.
   Robert came back so excited. Then every day he brought
   more and more photographs home. We became so close,
   incredibly close. Colin brought us together. It was my idea
   to put him here on the wall – so that we could see him – all
   the time, as we fucked.
   MARY *rubs her legs.* CAROLINE *points to a photograph of*
   COLIN *naked, prone on a bed.*
   I took that one myself. Isn't it brilliant?
   MARY *tries to speak.*
MARY: Why? (*She struggles with the word.*) Why?
CAROLINE: Then Robert brought you home. It was as if God
   was in on our dream. I knew that fantasy was passing into
   reality. Have you ever experienced that? It's like stepping
   into a mirror.
   MARY *attempts to say the word 'Colin'.*
   Wake up, what's the matter with you? Robert and Colin
   are back. Do you know where we are now? Shall I tell you?
   She takes MARY's *head in her hands and whispers into her
   ear.*
   We're on the other side of the mirror.

INT. APARTMENT. GALLERY. EVENING
ROBERT *opening champagne.* COLIN *standing with glasses.*

CAROLINE *and* MARY *come in.* MARY *is stumbling, one hand on*
CAROLINE'*s shoulder.*

COLIN: Mary, what is it?

The cork pops.

ROBERT: Glasses.

COLIN *holds out the glasses.* ROBERT *pours.*

CAROLINE *seats* MARY. COLIN *goes to her.*

COLIN: Mary, what is it? What's the matter?

ROBERT: Cheers.

CAROLINE: It's a mild touch of sunstroke. That's all.

COLIN *takes* MARY'*s hand.*

COLIN: She's not hot. (*To* MARY) What is it? Is it sunstroke?

MARY *tries to speak.*

Tell me. Try to tell me.

She manages a strangled hard 'C'.

Are you saying my name?

She pants. She holds his hand tightly. She manages to say:

MARY: G . . . G . . . Go . . .

ROBERT: Cold. She's cold.

CAROLINE: We shouldn't crowd her.

COLIN: She needs a doctor.

He moves away.

Where's your telephone?

CAROLINE: It's been disconnected.

COLIN: Disconnected?

CAROLINE: We're going away.

COLIN: Well, you must know a doctor! Go and fetch a doctor!
She's very ill.

ROBERT *and* CAROLINE *link hands and walk towards him.*

ROBERT: No need to shout.

CAROLINE: She'll be fine.

COLIN *retreats, knocks the champagne bottle over. It falls and*
spills.

ROBERT: What a waste.

COLIN'*s back is against the glass door.*

ROBERT *puts an arm against the window, boxing* COLIN *in.*

CAROLINE *strokes his cheek.*

CAROLINE: Mary understands. You understand too, don't you?
You understand. You do understand. Don't you?

47

She pulls his shirt out from his jeans and strokes his stomach.
From outside voices and sounds drift up; gondoliers.
COLIN *springs forward, banging* CAROLINE'*s face with his*
forearm. He runs towards MARY.
ROBERT *moves quickly, bends, grasps* COLIN'*s ankle, tips him*
on to the floor. He picks him up by an arm and a leg, drags
him to the wall, stands him up and slams him against the wall,
holding him with one hand at his throat.
Silence.
You've cut my lip.
She collects the blood from her lip and daubs COLIN'*s mouth*
with it.

COLIN: What have you done to Mary? Look. I'll do anything
you want – but get a doctor for her. Do you hear? I'll do
what you want. What do you want?

ROBERT: Want? I'll show you what we want.
CAROLINE *kisses* COLIN. *He wrenches away and spits in her*
face.

CAROLINE: Silly boy.
She starts to undo COLIN'*s jeans. She caresses him.* ROBERT *is*
still holding him by the throat. With his other hand he takes a
razor from his pocket and flicks it open.

ROBERT: I'll show you.

MARY'S POINT OF VIEW
An unfocused mating dance with three figures.
Sudden flash of razor blade.
Blood.
ROBERT *and* CAROLINE *kissing.*

COLIN AGAINST THE WALL
COLIN *begins to slide slowly down the wall to the floor. His eyes are*
glazed. His body twitches.

COLIN: (*Emptily*) Mary?

MARY STARING
Over her face, excited incoherent whispers, gasps, moans, whimpers,
giggles.
These sounds fade away to silence.
The screen darkens. MARY'*s eyes in nightlight. Sound of distant dogs.*

48

Slowly the light grows and changes on MARY's *face. It becomes morning. Growing sounds of distant radios and motorboats. Sunlight.*

APARTMENT. MORNING
MARY *sitting still in her chair.*
COLIN's *body slumped by the wall, shrunken.*
An open razor. A large bloodstain on the floor.
The luggage by the door has gone.

MARY STARING
A POLICEMAN's *voice-over.*
POLICEMAN: (*Voice over*) What did you want from these
    people?
    Pause.
    I ask you again. What did you want from these people?

INT. POLICE STATION. DAY
MARY *sitting with two* POLICEMEN. MARY *speaks vacantly,*
without emotion.
MARY: Nothing. They were friends.
POLICEMAN: Friends?
MARY: We had dinner there.
POLICEMAN: Why did you go back with your boyfriend to these
    people?
    Pause.
    What did you want from them?
    She stares at him.
    Did your boyfriend like the woman?
MARY: I liked her . . . I don't think he . . .
POLICEMAN: Did your boyfriend like the man?
MARY: No. No, he didn't.
POLICEMAN: And you? You liked the man? Did you like the
    man?
    She stares at him.
MARY: No.
POLICEMAN: So why did you go to dinner? And why did you go
    back? For more dinner?
    She stares at him.

SECOND POLICEMAN: Why did you come to Venice? What were
    you looking for?
MARY: Nothing. We . . .
SECOND POLICEMAN: Were you looking for some fun?
MARY: We were going to get married.
    Silence.
    The FIRST POLICEMAN *stamps a document and gives it to
    her.*

INT. POLICE STATION. MORTUARY
COLIN's *body on a bench. A* POLICEMAN *and* MARY.
POLICEMAN: Is this the body of Colin Mayhew?
MARY: Yes.
POLICEMAN: Sign here.
    She signs a document.
MARY: They've combed his hair the wrong way.
POLICEMAN: Sorry?
MARY: It doesn't go that way.
    She starts to comb COLIN's *hair with her fingers.*
    It goes this way.

INT. POLICE STATION. CORRIDOR
MARY *and* POLICEMAN *walking down the corridor.*
They pass doors with circular windows looking into the rooms.
In one room CAROLINE *is sitting quite still, looking out of a
window.*
In the next room ROBERT *is sitting at a table with two detectives.*
MARY *walks on.*
*The camera stops at the window of Robert's room and slowly goes
in.*

INT. INTERVIEW ROOM
The DETECTIVES *and* ROBERT.
DETECTIVE: We don't get it. You plan everything in advance –
    you prepare everything – you sell your bar – you sell the
    apartment – you buy the drug – and so on and so on – but
    then on the other hand you leave your razor with your own
    fingerprints – you book tickets under your own name and
    you travel on your own passport – we don't get it.

ROBERT: Listen. I'll tell you what it is. (*He smiles.*) Let me tell you something.
He looks at them both.
My father was a very big man. All his life he wore a black moustache. When it turned grey he used a little brush to keep it black, such as ladies use for their eyes. Mascara.
He sits, staring at the detectives.

Reunion

Reunion was produced in 1989. The cast included:

HENRY	Jason Robards
HANS STRAUSS	Christian Anholt
KONRADIN VON LOHENBURG	Samuel West
GRÄFIN VON LOHENBURG	Françoise Fabian
LISA, Henry's daughter	Maureen Kerwin
HERR VON LOHENBURG, Konradin's father	Jacques Brunet
MRS STRAUSS, Hans's mother	Barbara Jefford
HERR STRAUSS, Hans's father	Bert Parnaby

Director	Jerry Schatzberg
Producer	Vincent Malle
Production Designer	Alexandre Trauner
Director of Photography	Bruno de Keyzer
Costume Designer	David Perry
Editor	Martine Barraque
Music	Philippe Sarde

EXT. A PRISON YARD. DAY
Black and white film.
A line of men marching towards a door. They are naked to the
waist, some holding their trousers up.
German guards accompany them.
They file through the door into a room. The camera stays at the open
door.

INT. EXECUTION ROOM. DAY
The room is bare. Two windows at the back. Winter sunshine
slanting in. A rafter along the ceiling in front of the window.
Butcher's hooks hanging down.
A tall man in SS uniform stands straight-backed by the window.
The men file in and stand along the wall.
The door closes with a clang.

EXT. BAUER HOUSE: GARDEN (1932). DAY
Silent shot. A little girl on a swing under a tree, pushed by her
father. In background two other children.

INT. SCHOOLROOM (1932). DAY
Silent shot. KONRADIN *(sixteen) entering the room and standing.*
The class looking at him. HANS *(Henry when sixteen) looks up.*
Sounds of Central Park gradually grow on the soundtrack. Barking
dogs.

EXT. CENTRAL PARK, NEW YORK (1987). SUMMER. DAY
HENRY *(aged seventy) sitting on a park bench, looking into space.*
He is casually dressed.
A little girl, ALEX *(aged five), playing with a ball on the grass. The*
ball bounces away. She follows it. Two large dogs charge down the
hill towards her. She sees them, cries out, falls. The dogs swerve
away. She sits, crying.
HENRY *hears her cries. He stands, looks about him in panic, sees*
her, stumbles down the grass verge towards her.

He takes her in his arms.

HENRY: Alex, Alex, it's all right, I'm here, it's all right, I'm here.

INT. HENRY'S LAW OFFICE. DAY

Activity up and down corridors, telephones ringing, etc.

HENRY *in his office on the phone. He wears a dark suit.*

HENRY: (*Into phone*) Tell him we can handle that. Sure. See I have the papers here by Wednesday . . . I'm back Thursday . . . Just have it on my desk for when I get back. We'll give 'em hell . . . What? . . . Germany. . . . Oh yeah? You fought there? Which side were you on? (*He laughs.*) Say no more. Sure, sure. I'll give them all your love. Bye.

He puts the phone down. His SECRETARY *comes to the desk.*

SECRETARY: Here's your ticket. And your travellers' cheques. And some cash.

HENRY: Uh-huh.

She puts them in a leather wallet.

SECRETARY: And here's the inventory.

He takes it. We glimpse a typed list in German.

HENRY: OK.

He puts it into the wallet. The SECRETARY *smiles.*

SECRETARY: And that's it.

HENRY: Good. Fine.

INT. NEW YORK RESTAURANT. DAY

LISA (*in her thirties*) at a table. HENRY *sitting. He kisses her on the cheek.*

HENRY: How is she? Is she OK?

LISA: Sure she is.

HENRY: I got such a shock. You don't know how big they were – the dogs. I blame myself.

LISA: Dad, she's perfectly all right. She's forgotten all about it.

HENRY: It's just that I was . . . my mind was . . . I wasn't paying attention . . .

LISA: Listen. Why are you taking this trip?

HENRY: Why?

LISA: You don't have to go. You don't want to go. Why are you
   going?
HENRY: I have to take care of this . . . thing.
LISA: You could do it from here. You know that. Your secretary
   could do it for you. I could do it for you. You don't have to
   go all the way over there yourself. Do you? What's the
   point?
HENRY: I want to do it myself. I have to go and do it myself.
   He takes her hand.
   I'll be fine. Really. I'll be fine. I promise you. (*He smiles.*)
   I'm not a child.
WAITER: Are you going to have an aperitif before lunch, Mr
   Strauss?
HENRY: Sure. Give me a Bloody Mary. (*To* LISA) What about
   you?
LISA: I don't want anything.

INT. PARK AVENUE APARTMENT. DAY
The apartment is spacious, uncluttered.
Light slants through the wide windows. Traffic sounds, distant.
Stillness.
HENRY *is standing by the window, looking out. A man in*
chauffeur's uniform comes into the far end of the room, holding a
suitcase.
CHAUFFEUR: Ready, sir?
HENRY: What's the time?
CHAUFFEUR: Four o'clock.
HENRY: OK.
   He walks to the door.

SILENT FLASH.
HANS *swinging on horizontal bar.*

INT. KENNEDY AIRPORT. FIRST-CLASS CHECK-IN
Coming up on to a computer:
   Strauss, Henry
   Lufthansa 324
   New York–Stuttgart (return
   First class – Seat D3

57

SILENT FLASH
FATHER *in officer's uniform with sword and Iron Cross standing next to a Nazi.*

INT. PLANE
HENRY *sitting in first class.*
ANNOUNCEMENT: (*In German*) Captain Richter and his crew
    welcome you aboard this Lufthansa flight to Stuttgart.
    Your flight time will be –

SILENT FLASH
Marlene Dietrich crossing her legs in The Blue Angel.

INT. STUTTGART. HOTEL AM SCHLOSSGARTEN. RECEPTION
RECEPTIONIST: Mr Strauss. Yes indeed. Thank you very much.
    Room 654. Have a nice stay, Mr Strauss.
    Another MAN *escorts* HENRY *to the elevator.*
MAN: Is this your first time in Stuttgart?
HENRY: No.

INT. HOTEL BEDROOM. STUTTGART. NIGHT
*Henry standing, looking about the room. He switches on the
television set. A discussion programme. Henry opens his suitcase. He
starts to unpack. On the screen the* PRESENTER *is talking to a studio
filled with young people (in German).*
PRESENTER: Now look at this.
    Laurence Olivier in Henry V *comes up on the screen.*
OLIVIER: Then will he strip his sleeve and show his scars,
      And say, 'These wounds I had on Crispin's day.'
      Old men forget; yet all shall be forgot,
      But he'll remember with advantages
      What feats he did that day. Then shall our names,
      Familiar in his mouth as household words,
      Harry the king, Bedford and Exeter,
      Warwick and Talbot, Salisbury and Gloucester,
      Be in their flowing cups freshly remember'd.
    The clip ends. The PRESENTER *speaks.*
PRESENTER: Now what was Laurence Olivier doing? Laurence

Olivier was acting a man who is himself acting – who is putting on an act.

HENRY *goes into the bathroom.*

INT. HOTEL BATHROOM. DAY

HENRY *unpacking his shaving materials.*

PRESENTER: (*Voice over*) Henry the Fifth actually feels very uncertain indeed about the battle ahead but is able to hide this uncertainty by putting on a mask – by acting! Now here is a quite different case. Or is it?

Suddenly the voice of JUDGE FREISLER *screaming.* HENRY *stops unpacking and, suddenly riveted, stares into the mirror. He goes into the other room.*

INT. HOTEL BEDROOM. DAY

JUDGE FREISLER *on the television screen screaming. Black and white.*

PRESENTER: (*Voice over*) Now that man – is he an actor? Is he acting? Is he simply playing the part of a cruel and sadistic judge? Or is he real? Is he the real thing?

HENRY *switches the television set off abruptly.*

INT. HOTEL BAR. EARLY EVENING

HENRY *comes into the bar. It is empty apart from a Japanese* BUSINESSMAN *and the* BARTENDER. *They are talking.*

BARTENDER: Yes, in Hanau. A very big company.

BUSINESSMAN: Oh yes. I know. But in Japan too. In Japan it is advancing very fast.

HENRY: A beer. Dutch. You have Dutch beer?

The BARTENDER *shrugs.*

BARTENDER: Yes.

He opens the bottle of beer.

BUSINESSMAN: You are American?

HENRY: Yes.

BUSINESSMAN: You are also developing superconductors in America.

HENRY: Superconductors?

BUSINESSMAN: Sure. They're going to revolutionize electronics. We were just talking about it. You don't know about them?

HENRY: No.

BUSINESSMAN: They're going to change the world. Automobiles
will run on electric magnets. Pollution will be finished. It
will be a beautiful new, clean world. Listen – it's not going
to just change the world, it's going to save the world. We're
going to save the damn world and we're going to make a lot
of damn big money. Believe me. You should get into it
now. Take my advice. You can't lose.

The BARTENDER *leans across the bar to* HENRY, *smiling.*

BARTENDER: It will be good for Germany too.

EXT. HOTEL AM SCHLOSSGARTEN. NIGHT

HENRY *comes out of the hotel and walks into the park. A group of
winos on a park bench with bottles. He approaches the Opera House
and stops to look at it. It is brightly lit.*

EXT. SHOPPING ARCADE. NIGHT

HENRY *walking through the arcade. He passes a shop window
containing guns of all sizes. A tramp sits on a doorstep shouting. He
looks across the arcade at a McDonald's hamburger restaurant. A
group of punks eating.*

INT. HOTEL RECEPTION. MORNING

HENRY *at the desk.*

HENRY: What flights are there tonight for New York?

RECEPTIONIST: New York?

HENRY: Yes.

RECEPTIONIST: Your room?

HENRY: 654. Strauss.

She looks at the computer.

RECEPTIONIST: But you have reserved your room until
Wednesday.

HENRY: I know. But I want to know what flights there are
tonight.

RECEPTIONIST: The same as Wednesday. The same as every
night.

HENRY: I see.

He turns and goes out of the hotel.

60

EXT. WIDE ROAD. STUTTGART. DAY

HENRY *walks towards the corner, stops, looks about. At the corner is a tall office block. An elderly man approaches.* HENRY *stops him.*

HENRY: Excuse me. Do you speak any English?

The MAN *stares at him.*

MAN: Little. A little.

HENRY: You are from Stuttgart?

MAN: Oh yes. Yes.

HENRY: Was there a school here? At this corner? The Karl Alexander Gymnasium? Was it here?

MAN: Bombed. (*He gestures.*) Kaputt. Gone.

HENRY: Thank you.

The MAN *clicks his heels, bows.*

MAN: (*In German*) At your service.

INT. TRAVELLING TAXI. DAY

HENRY *looking out. Radio playing.*

EXT. MODERN STUTTGART

HENRY's *point of view.*

INT. WAREHOUSE OFFICE

A MAN *at a desk.* HENRY *sitting at the desk. The* MAN *is looking at a file.*

MAN: Strauss. Yes.

He looks up for a moment at HENRY *and then picks up the phone.*

In German) Herr Strauss is here. Lot 415. (*To* HENRY) Follow me please.

They go out into the corridor.

Go down there, please. Take the elevator to the fifth floor. Someone is waiting.

HENRY: Thank you.

He begins to walk down the corridor.

INT. WAREHOUSE. FIFTH FLOOR

A MAN *removing sheets from furniture and tea chests.*

MAN: You will ring that bell when you have finished, please.

HENRY: Yes. Thank you.

HENRY *walks slowly through the furniture: heavy oak chairs,*
tables, dressing tables, etc. He rummages in a tea chest,
unwrapping German newspaper. He looks at the date – 1934.
He brings out a long-stemmed wine glass, blue Meissen plates,
a Jewish candlestick.
From another tea chest he unwraps Cézanne and Van Gogh
prints and some books. Following this, coins, a tiger's claw, a
Roman fibula, an elephant's back tooth. A Corinthian coin.
He looks carefully at the coin and slips it into his pocket.
He goes to the next tea chest and unwraps an Iron Cross and an
officer's sword. He stares at them.

INT. WAREHOUSE OFFICE
HENRY *with* MAN.
MAN: OK?
HENRY: It's all in very good condition.
MAN: Yes, I think so.
HENRY: I want you to sell it and I want the money to go to
    charity.
MAN: Yes, if you wish. What charity?
HENRY: Oh . . .
MAN: There are hundreds of charities. You have a preference?
HENRY: The blind.
    The MAN *writes, murmurs.*
MAN: The blind.

INT. SCHOOLROOM (1932)
Silent shot. Slow motion.
KONRADIN *(sixteen) entering the room and standing.*

EXT. A LAKE. DAY
At the far side of the lake a procession with banners. A chorus of
voices singing in the distance.

INT. SCHOOLROOM (1932)
Boys at their desks, including HANS, *are looking up, staring at*
KONRADIN.
The HEADMASTER *whispers in* HERR ZIMMERMAN'S *ear and goes*
out.

KONRADIN *stands still. He wears a light-grey suit, pale-blue shirt,*
dark-blue tie.

HERR ZIMMERMAN *shows* KONRADIN *to a desk and walks*
backwards to his own chair. KONRADIN *sits.*

HERR ZIMMERMAN: Would you please give me your surname,
 Christian name and the date and place of your birth.
 KONRADIN *stands.*

KONRADIN: Graf von Lohenburg. Konradin. Born 19th of
 January 1916. Burg Lohenburg. Württemberg.
 He sits.

THE BOYS
The boys, scruffy, untidy, ink-stained, stare at KONRADIN, *who sits*
erect and composed, elegant.

HANS WATCHING KONRADIN

KONRADIN AT HIS DESK
KONRADIN *taking pencils from his briefcase. His fingers: long,*
clean.

EXT. SCHOOLYARD. DAY
Flag-raising ceremony. The school at attention. The ceremony ends.
Two boys approach KONRADIN. *One clicks his heels.* HANS *is in the*
background.

VON HANKHOFEN: Lohenburg. Baron von Hankhofen. How do
 you do?

KONRADIN: How do you do?

VON HANKHOFEN: May I introduce you to Prince Hubertus
 Petershagen Wildenheim?
 THE PRINCE *clicks his heels and bows.*

THE PRINCE: How do you do?

KONRADIN: How do you do?

THE PRINCE: I believe you know my cousin – Count Dietrich
 Petershagen Wildenheim?

KONRADIN: Dietrich?

THE PRINCE: You stayed at his father's castle at Wimpfen-am-
 Neckar.

VON HANKHOFEN: Duke Eberhard Ludwig was shooting there.

KONRADIN: No, no, I'm afraid your cousin is confusing me with
somebody else.

THE PRINCE: Somebody else?

KONRADIN: Somebody who looks like me perhaps?

He grins, turns and walks into school. THE PRINCE *and*
BARON *look at each other.* HANS *studies them.*

INT. SCHOOL CLOAKROOM. AFTERNOON

Boys milling about. HANS *packing his case. Through the window*
KONRADIN *seen walking to the school gates.* HANS *looks after him.*

INT. STRAUSS HOUSE. PARLOUR. DAY

HANS *drinking tea.*

DR STRAUSS: One of the oldest families in Germany. They go
back to the twelfth century. Look them up in the
encyclopaedia. Very, very distinguished. Warriors. Great
German warriors.

HANS: What were our ancestors – I mean in the twelfth century?

DR STRAUSS: Cattle dealers.

HANS: Distinguished?

DR STRAUSS: (*Smiling*) I don't imagine they were all that close to
the Emperor.

They drink their tea.

What's he like, your friend?

HANS: He's not my friend. Anyway, he keeps himself to
himself. Which suits me.

INT. GYM

*The class running round the gym, with exhortations from the gym
instructor,* 'MUSCLE MAX'.

MUSCLE MAX: Right! Stop! Stand easy. Now watch this.

*He goes to the horizontal bar, stands to attention under it,
stretches up his arms and then jumps. He raises his body slowly
inch by inch, then turns to the right, to the left, etc. He then
swings faster and faster and lands lightly on his toes.*

Right! Were you watching?

THE CLASS: Yes, sir.

MUSCLE MAX: Who's going to be the first volunteer?

HANS: Me, sir.

MUSCLE MAX: You? All right, come on then.

> HANS *goes to the bar. He jumps up and grasps the rod.*
> *He raises his body from right to left and from left to right,*
> *hangs on his knees, swings upwards and rests for a second on*
> *the bar, then swings faster and faster, jumps over the bar and*
> *lands on his feet.*
> *During all this* KONRADIN'S *eyes have not left him.*
> *As he lands there is surprised laughter from some of the boys,*
> *applause from others.*

Good, Strauss. I didn't know you had it in you.

> HANS'S *and* KONRADIN'S *eyes meet.*

INT. SCHOOLROOM. MORNING

HANS *taking some Greek coins from his briefcase. He studies them*
through a magnifying glass. In background KONRADIN *watching.*
KONRADIN *strolls across to* HANS'S *desk.*

KONRADIN: Greek?

HANS: Yes.

KONRADIN: I collect too. May I look?

> HANS *gives him the magnifying glass.* KONRADIN *looks*
> *through it.*

Yes, Pallas Athena. I have it. Who's this?

HANS: Alexander the Great.

> *The* MASTER *walks in, bangs on his desk with a ruler.*

MASTER: Good morning. Everybody sit down.

> KONRADIN *goes to his desk.*

EXT. SCHOOL GROUNDS. DAY

REUTTER, MÜLLER *and* FRANK *approach* KONRADIN. HANS *is in*
the background, reading.

REUTTER: Lohenburg, I'm not sure that you know what we
three are known as?

KONRADIN: No. What?

REUTTER: The Caviar of the class.

KONRADIN: Oh? Why?

MÜLLER: (*Grinning*) Because we're the most intelligent, well-
read, knowledgeable and artistic people in the class.

KONRADIN: Good lord. Are you really?

FRANK: Oh yes, there's no doubt about it. You can ask anyone.

KONRADIN: Oh? Who shall I ask?

FRANK: Us!

He laughs.

REUTTER: The thing is, we'd like to invite you to take part in a play-reading we're giving on Thursday – to a rather select audience.

KONRADIN: What's the play?

MÜLLER: *Hamlet.*

FRANK: We thought you might like to read the part of the Prince yourself.

KONRADIN: But I'm not an actor, I'm afraid. And I've never understood *Hamlet.* And anyway I'm very busy these days. So sorry.

KONRADIN *turns and walks away, glancing at* HANS.

INT. SCHOOLROOM. DAY

HANS *standing addressing the class.*

HANS: Hamlet is a classic example of schizophrenia, of split personality. On the one hand, he laments the deterioration of civilized values, the decline in standards, the breakdown of moral systems, the failure of the state – and on the other hand he treats people like rubbish, kills Polonius without a sign of remorse, is vicious to his mother, drives Ophelia crazy, coldly sends Rosencrantz and Guildenstern to their deaths. The great Sigmund Freud would describe this as a classic case of schizophrenia.

BOLLACHER *mutters in a low voice.*

BOLLACHER: Sigmund Freud! Sigmund Freud is a Jew!

Silence.

HANS *turns slowly and looks at* BOLLACHER.

MASTER: Thank you, Strauss. Very interesting.

INT. GYM. DAY

Six boys swinging from rings throwing medicine balls at lines of pins.

BOLLACHER *tying his shoelaces.* HANS *throws his ball at*

BOLLACHER. *It hits him on the head.* BOLLACHER *turns angrily.*
HANS *continues to swing.*

EXT. STUTTGART STREET. DAY
KONRADIN *walking.* HANS *walking a way behind him.* KONRADIN
slows. HANS *slows.* HANS *accelerates, passes* KONRADIN, *nods
perfunctorily, walks on.*
KONRADIN *calls after him.*
KONRADIN: Hello!
    HANS *turns.* KONRADIN *catches him up.*
    Which way are you going?
HANS: Karalshohe.
KONRADIN: We're going the same way.
    They walk.
    Who's Freud?
HANS: Didn't you hear what Bollacher said? He's a Jew.
KONRADIN: No, apart from that.
HANS: You mean you haven't heard of him?
KONRADIN: Well, vaguely. What is he exactly?
HANS: Well . . . he's a doctor. Of the mind. He writes books
    about the mind.
KONRADIN: Oh.
    They walk on.
    Are they any good?
HANS: Terrific. I haven't read all of them, of course.
    They walk on.
    What do you think of the school?
KONRADIN: Well . . . I don't know, really. I can't compare it
    with any other, you see.
HANS: Why not?
KONRADIN: (*Laughing*) I've never been to school before!
    Pathetic, isn't it? I've only ever had private tutors.
HANS: Really? Why?
KONRADIN: Well . . . my father was Ambassador – first to
    Brazil – and then to Turkey. So . . . I had these tutors.
HANS: Ah.
    They walk on.
KONRADIN: What do *you* think of the school?

HANS: I can't wait to get to university and meet some girls.
They laugh and walk on.

STUTTGART STREET
High shot of the two boys walking up a hill, talking vigorously.

EXT. KONRADIN'S HOUSE. DAY
The boys walking towards the house, talking.
KONRADIN: I think America might be good. Yale University.
Have you heard of it?
HANS: Of course. But how's your English?
KONRADIN: Not bad.
They stop at a pair of great gates.
I live here. (*He extends his hand.*) See you tomorrow.
They shake hands. KONRADIN *opens the heavy gate and walks
up the oleander-bordered path towards an arch. Through the
arch can be seen the lower level of a double staircase.* HANS
watches KONRADIN *disappear.* HANS *turns away and begins to
run up the hill.*

EXT. BAUER HOUSE. GARDEN. DAY
The Bauer children playing on the swing. HANS *passes on his way to
his own house. He waves at the children. They wave back.* HANS
goes into his house.

INT. STRAUSS HOUSE. DAY
HANS *comes in the front door. He hears two voices from the sitting-
room. His* FATHER *and another man. He stops, listens.*
FATHER: But what kind of claim is that? It doesn't make any
sense!
ZIONIST: It's our homeland. Palestine is our homeland.
FATHER: What, after two thousand years?
ZIONIST: Yes.
FATHER: But it's absolutely ridiculous! It's as if . . . it's as if
Italy claimed Germany because it was once occupied by the
Romans!
ZIONIST: No it isn't.
FATHER: Anyway I was born in Stuttgart – not Jerusalem.
ZIONIST: And what about Hitler?

FATHER: A temporary illness – like measles. Once the economic situation improves Hitler will go out of fashion. He won't be necessary. Can't you see that? I know the German people. This is the land of Goethe, of Schiller, of Beethoven! They're not going to fall for that rubbish.

ZIONIST: And the Jews?

FATHER: Twelve thousand Jews died for Germany in the last war! Proudly! I was wounded twice! I have the honour to tell you I was awarded the Iron Cross first class by my country. Yes – I'm proud to be a Jew – but I'm also proud to be a German!

ZIONIST: You're a Jew? What kind of Jew?

FATHER: A German Jew! We go to synagogue on Yom Kippur and we sing 'Silent Night' at Christmas.

ZIONIST: You're mad.

The ZIONIST *comes out into the hall fastening his briefcase. He sees* HANS *and points back into the room.*
He's mad.
He leaves the house. HANS *goes into the sitting-room.*

INT. SITTING-ROOM. DAY

FATHER: They're such dangerous fools, these people!

MOTHER: Hello, Hans.

HANS: I just walked up the hill with Lohenburg.

FATHER: So narrow-minded! It drives me mad!

MOTHER: Why do you get so excited?

FATHER: Excited! It's a serious matter, that's why! These people can't think. They're just panicking. They're distorting the truth. They have everything totally out of proportion. All they do is make things worse!

MOTHER: You have a dozen patients waiting for you. They've been sitting in your office for twenty minutes.

FATHER: Yes, yes. (*To* HANS) How's school?

HANS: All right.

FATHER *stands a moment and then speaks quietly.*

FATHER: I would like to remind you of what happened on my fiftieth birthday. (*He looks at them both.*) Do you remember? I'll tell you. The Mayor of this town gave a reception for me at the town hall. You were both at my

69

side. They played *Eine kleine Nachtmusik* in my honour. It was a splendid occasion. They wished to show their respect for me and they did so. Their respect for a German Jew. Remember that.

He leaves the room.

MOTHER *turns to* HANS.

MOTHER: What's he like? Is he nice?

HANS: Who?

MOTHER: Lohenburg.

HANS: Oh, he's all right. It's nothing to make a fuss about. We're not friends or anything.

EXT. SCHOOL YARD. MORNING

Boys milling. HANS *stands alone.* KONRADIN *enters the yard, looks about, sees* HANS, *walks through the crowd towards him. They shake hands. Boys turn and stare.*

The bell rings. KONRADIN *and* HANS *go into the school together, ignoring the others.*

Outside the school walls a Nazi truck goes by.

VOICE: (*Through the loudspeaker*) Vote for the National Socialist Party! Vote for the National Socialist Party!

HANS *and* KONRADIN *seen through coffee-shop window, talking earnestly.*

HANS *and* KONRADIN *standing in doorway, talking, laughing. Pouring rain.*

HANS *and* KONRADIN *running downhill. Bright sun.*

INT. LIVING ROOM. DAY

Schubert Lieder *playing on a gramophone.*

Heavy oak furniture. Blue Meissen plates and long-stemmed wine glasses, purple and blue, on a dresser.

The camera pans across the room into a conservatory.

INT. CONSERVATORY. DAY

MOTHER *sitting under a rubber tree sewing. The front door closes. She lifts her head.*

MOTHER: (*Calling*) Hans?

HANS: (*Out of shot*) Mother!

> *The music continues.* HANS *and* KONRADIN *coming into the conservatory.*
>
> Mother, this is my friend Konradin von Lohenburg.
>
> *She smiles, gives* KONRADIN *her hand. He kisses it.*

MOTHER: Good afternoon, Konradin. I'm very happy to meet you.

KONRADIN: That's very kind of you, Mrs Strauss.

MOTHER: I hear you've lived in Turkey, South America . . . is that right?

KONRADIN: Oh yes. But I prefer Germany. I think the beauty of Germany is unbeatable.

HANS: We want to start making some trips into the Black Forest . . . seeing the country . . . on weekends . . . would that be all right?

MOTHER: Staying the night, you mean?

HANS: Yes.

MOTHER: Where?

KONRADIN: Oh . . . inns . . .

MOTHER: Well, I don't see why not. As you say, we do live in a very beautiful country. You should both . . . see as much of it as possible . . .

INT. LANDING

HANS *leading* KONRADIN *to his room.*

KONRADIN: What a charming woman, your mother.

> *They go into Hans's room.*

INT. HANS'S BEDROOM

The window looks down into the valley, the vineyards spreading across the hills.

KONRADIN *looks at the prints on the walls (Van Gogh, Cézanne, Japanese etchings) and then examines the books on the shelves (Goethe, Schiller, Kleist, Hölderlin, Rilke, Tolstoy, Dostoevsky, Lermontov, Pushkin, Turgenev, Gogol, Shakespeare, Byron, Baudelaire, Balzac, Flaubert, Stendhal, Verlaine, Rimbaud).*

KONRADIN: This is quite a library.

> *He stares at the Russian titles.*

The Russians aren't in the original, are they?

HANS *laughs*.

HANS: No! I haven't had time to learn Russian yet.

KONRADIN: Thank God for that. Should I read Dostoevsky?

HANS: You certainly should. He's tremendous. He's . . . I don't know . . . gigantic.

He takes a book from the shelves and gives it to KONRADIN. Here. *Crime and Punishment*. Start with that.

KONRADIN: Wonderful. Thanks.

HANS takes KONRADIN to a corner of the room to see his collection. KONRADIN examines the items with great interest. The collection consists of corals from the Red Sea, topazes, malachites, a Roman fibula, the iron point of a javelin, some Roman coins, a tiger's tooth.

Suddenly, DR STRAUSS's *voice is heard on the stairs.*

FATHER: (*Out of shot*) Hans.

He comes in, sees KONRADIN, clicks his heels, stands stiffly and puts out his hand.

How do you do? I am Dr Strauss.

KONRADIN *bows slightly. They shake hands.*

I am greatly honoured, Herr Graf, to have the scion of such an illustrious family under my roof. I have never had the pleasure of meeting your father, but I knew many of his friends, particularly Baron von Klumpf, who commanded the Second Squadron of the first Uhlan regiment, Ritter von Trompeda of the Hussars and Putzi von Grimmelshausen, known as 'Bautz'. I am sure your father must have told you of Bautz, who was a bosom friend of the Crown Prince? One day, so Bautz told me, his Imperial Highness, whose headquarters were then at Charlesroi, called for him and said to him, 'Bautz, my dear friend, I want to ask you a great favour. You know Gretel, my chimpanzee, is still a virgin and badly needs a husband. I want to arrange a wedding to which I will invite all my staff. Take your car and travel round Germany and find me a healthy, good-looking male.' Bautz clicked his heels, stood to attention and said, 'Jawohl, Imperial Highness.' Then he marched out, jumped into the Crown Prince's

Daimler and travelled from zoo to zoo, all over the country.
Finally a fortnight later he came back with an enormous
chimp called George V. There was a fabulous wedding,
everybody got drunk on champagne, George V and Gretel
were sent off into their cage for their honeymoon and Bautz
got the Ritterkreutz with oak leaves.

He roars with laughter.

HANS *and* KONRADIN *are silent.*

FATHER *clicks his heels.*

I do hope, Herr Graf, that in future you will look upon this
house as your second home. Please commend me to your
father.

He bows, leaves the room.

Silence.

KONRADIN *continues to examine the collection.* HANS *stands by
the window, his eyes closed, fists clenched.* KONRADIN *speaks
quietly.*

KONRADIN: This is a great collection. I like your room.

HANS *turns abruptly, looks at* KONRADIN *keenly.*

I really like it.

EXT. ROAD INTO BLACK FOREST. DAY

HANS *and* KONRADIN *cycling fast.*

EXT. CASTLE OVERLOOKING GORGE. DAY

Long shot. A white castle juts out from the hillside.

EXT. CASTLE TERRACE. DAY

HANS *and* KONRADIN *walk on to the terrace and look down into the
gorge.*

HANS *whistles.*

KONRADIN: It is true, isn't it? It is the most beautiful country in
the world.

HANS: Yes. It's true.

They look down.

Mind you, I haven't been anywhere else. Well – not really.

KONRADIN *grins.*

KONRADIN: Take my word for it.

EXT. A RIVER. DAY
HANS *and* KONRADIN *swimming, racing across the river. They*
reach the bank together.
KONRADIN: A dead heat!

EXT. SMALL MOUNTAIN TOWN. CAFÉ IN THE SQUARE. DAY
HANS *and* KONRADIN *eating ice-cream.*
A truck drives into the square carrying SA troopers. They get out and
begin to paste Nazi posters on the walls. They are fat and ugly.
They shout at each other. One trooper becomes entangled in a poster.
HANS *and* KONRADIN *laugh into their ice-cream.*

INT. SCHOOLROOM. DAY
The class writing an essay, heads bent over their desks. The MASTER
leaning back in his chair. Silence.
Gradually, from the street sounds of martial music through a
loudspeaker, shouting, marching feet. HANS *looks up and out of the*
window.
The MASTER *watches him.*
MASTER: Strauss! You're dreaming. What are you dreaming?
HANS: I wasn't dreaming, sir.
MASTER: Stop dreaming. Get on with your work. Concentrate.
   HANS *slowly looks down at his paper.*

CINEMA SCREEN. BLACK AND WHITE
Marlene Dietrich in The Blue Angel. *She is in her underwear. She*
crosses her legs.

EXT. BLACK FOREST ROAD. DAY
HANS *and* KONRADIN *cycling along the empty road.*
In a field they see a boy running after a girl. They fall into the grass.
HANS *and* KONRADIN *cycle on.*

EXT. BLACK FOREST. A RUINED CASTLE. DAY
A great dead tree rises up through the ruin. A church steeple can be
seen in the distance through a gap in the wall.
The boys walk towards the ruin and sit down.
They take packets of sandwiches from their knapsacks.
HANS: Have one of these.

KONRADIN: (*Taking a sandwich*) Thanks.

    They munch.

    You know . . . I don't know what we're going to do about this question of sexual desire. It's a terrible problem.

HANS: Yes. The trouble is, I just don't know any girls. How about you?

KONRADIN: Not really. Only cousins.

    They sit, munching.

    Delicious sandwich. What is it?

HANS: Chicken.

KONRADIN: Wonderful flavour. Honestly. I've never tasted chicken like it.

HANS: Of course, sexual desire is just an appetite like anything else. And sexual intercourse is the appetite satisfied.

KONRADIN: You mean it's like eating this sandwich?

HANS: Exactly!

    They laugh.

    Church bells suddenly begin to ring. They look up at the church spire.

    Do you feel anything . . . ? When you hear those bells?

KONRADIN: Yes. I feel something.

HANS: What? What do you feel?

KONRADIN: Oh . . . you know . . . something . . .

    Pause.

    What about you? Do you feel anything?

HANS: Aah . . . Yes . . . I think I do.

INT. INN. BEDROOM. NIGHT

The boys lying in their beds. Moonlight.

KONRADIN: Tell me . . .

HANS: What?

KONRADIN: You remember this afternoon – when we were standing in the chapel – you said you felt something.

HANS: Yes.

KONRADIN: What was it? What did you feel?

    HANS *thinks.*

HANS: God knows.

    They burst into laughter, gradually subside.

KONRADIN: I've never had a friend before, you know. I mean, I have parents, relations – I know other people – but you're my first friend.

EXT. KONRADIN'S HOUSE. DAY

KONRADIN *and* HANS *walking towards the house, knapsacks on their backs. They stop at the gates.*

KONRADIN: Great trip.

HANS: It certainly was.

KONRADIN: (*Casually*) Like to come in and see my room?

HANS: Oh. Yes.

> *They go through the gate and walk down the drive towards the arch.* HANS *looks around the sees stables to his left. They pass under the arch.* HANS *looks up at the villa, which is set high above the ground and at the double staircases that lead up to the terrace. They begin to climb up towards the villa. They arrive at the main door.* KONRADIN *knocks lightly. The door opens. A servant lets them in, bows.*
>
> KONRADIN *leads* HANS *up the wide staircase. Oak-panelled walls, pictures of bear hunts, fighting stags, portraits of ancestors, etc.*
>
> *One door open. A lady's bedroom. A four-poster bed. White curtains moving in the breeze. On a dressing-table* HANS *glimpses bottles of scent, tortoiseshell brushes inlaid with silver, photographs in silver frames. His glance focuses on one photograph which has a striking resemblance to Adolf Hitler.*

KONRADIN: Up another flight I'm afraid.

> *They go on.*

INT. KONRADIN'S ROOM

View from the window of a large garden with a fountain and a small Doric temple.

KONRADIN: Here's my collection.

> *He takes out of cotton-wool Greek coins, a pegasus from Corinth, a minotaur from Knossos, a goddess from Gella, a glass bowl from Syria, a jade Roman vase, a Greek bronze figure of Hercules. A Corinthian coin.* HANS *examines the objects carefully, looks at* KONRADIN *and smiles.*

HANS: Fantastic.

> KONRADIN *picks up the Corinthian coin.*

KONRADIN: Why don't you have this?

HANS: Have it?

KONRADIN: Yes. Keep it. As a present.

 HANS *takes the coin and looks at it.*

HANS: Thanks.

EXT. SMALL GERMAN TOWN. RAILWAY STATION PLATFORM.
DAY

A train arriving. A great bell is clanging on the face of the engine.

GERTRUDE *(eighteen) standing on the platform. The train stops.*

KONRADIN *and* HANS *get out. They approach* GERTRUDE.

KONRADIN: Gertrude, may I introduce Hans Strauss. (*To* HANS)
 The Gräfin von Zeilarn, my cousin.

 HANS *bows and kisses her hand.*

EXT. RAILWAY STATION FORECOURT. DAY

*Nazi posters on the walls. Swastikas. The Hammer and Sickle. A
pony and trap stands.* GERTRUDE *and the boys get into it. The
driver flicks his whip and trots off.*

EXT. NARROW COUNTRY ROAD. DAY

*The pony and trap. Suddenly round a corner a group of Hitler
Youth appears, marching. The driver slows the trap. The group
marches past.*

GERTRUDE: Aren't they handsome!

KONRADIN: Would you say so?

GERTRUDE: Well, I've just said so.

 The trap drives on.

KONRADIN: I think they're pretty boneheaded.

GERTRUDE: Do you?

HANS: It's quite possible to be boneheaded and handsome at the
 same time, isn't it?

GERTRUDE: What do you mean by boneheaded?

KONRADIN: Unintelligent.

GERTRUDE: Not like you, you mean?

KONRADIN: Quite. Not like us.

GERTRUDE: Well, why don't you both join the Hitler Youth
 yourselves – so that it can benefit from your intelligence?

 KONRADIN *laughs, winks at* HANS.

77

EXT. ZEILARN ESTATE. DAY

GERTRUDE, KONRADIN *and* HANS *on the grass. The remains of the picnic. A servant stands by a table.*

GERTRUDE: (*To* KONRADIN) Where are you going for the summer?

KONRADIN: I think Sicily. And you?

GERTRUDE: (*Shrugging*) Oh . . . Baden Baden.
> *She turns to* HANS.
> Where do you go?

HANS: We're going to Switzerland.

GERTRUDE: Really? I'd be careful if I were you. I hear lots of rich Jews go to Switzerland to stuff themselves with Swiss cheese.
> *Silence.*

KONRADIN: Hans is Jewish.

HANS: But I'm not rich.

GERTRUDE: You're Jewish?

HANS: Yes.

GERTRUDE: But you don't look it!

HANS: Don't I?
> GERTRUDE *giggles, puts a hand to her mouth.*

GERTRUDE: Oh dear . . . I see why you haven't joined the Hitler Youth!

KONRADIN: Are you falling in love with the Nazis, Gertrude?

GERTRUDE: Well, it's all pretty exciting, don't you think? I mean, don't you feel the new spirit in Germany? You feel it everywhere. Anyway, I think they have the good of Germany at heart. I really do. So does Daddy. And Mummy.
> *In the distance, by an orchard, two riders on horseback appear.*
> GERTRUDE *looks up.*
> Oh look, there they are. I must go.
> *She stands. The boys stand.*
> (*To* HANS) Glad to meet you. But are you absolutely sure you're Jewish? You really don't look it.
> *She smiles, waves, walks away across the lawn towards the orchard.*
> KONRADIN *and* HANS *walk towards the gate.*

HANS: (*To* KONRADIN) Don't I look Jewish?

KONRADIN: No, I don't think you do.

HANS: But what does a Jew look like?

> *Laughter from the orchard. They turn and look.* GERTRUDE
> *with her parents.* GERTRUDE *waves. The parents do not.*

PONY AND TRAP TRAVELLING

KONRADIN *and* HANS *sitting, looking at the countryside.*

EXT. STREET. DUSK

HANS *and* KONRADIN *approaching* HANS's *house.*
They see smoke rising from the house next door (the Bauer house).
They stop and look at each other.

HANS: What's that?

> *They run towards the house, stop and stare. The Bauer house is*
> *a burnt-out ruin.*
> *They run towards the Strauss house.*

INT. STRAUSS HOUSE. HALL. DAY

HANS *and* KONRADIN *come through the front door into the hall.*
They hear sobbing. They stop. The sobbing continues. MOTHER
comes out of the sitting-room and goes to them. Her face is drained.

MOTHER: A tragedy. A tragedy.

HANS: What?

MOTHER: The children . . . the children . . . they died.

HANS: Died?

> *A further burst of sobbing from the sitting-room.*
> But . . . how . . . did someone . . . do it?

MOTHER: No. No one did it. It was an accident. No one did it.

> *She cries, softly.*
> No one did it.

EXT. BAUER HOUSE, SMOKING. DAY

HANS *and* KONRADIN *walking slowly through the garden towards*
the house.
The charred ropes of the swing dangle from the burnt tree.
They walk slowly through the wreckage (blackened walls, burnt
furniture, burnt toys). They stand in silence.

HANS: I knew these children.

> *Pause.*

KONRADIN: It's terrible.

HANS: God doesn't exist. How can he exist?

KONRADIN: These . . . things . . . these catastrophes . . . have happened . . . throughout history . . .

HANS: So what? How can this God allow three innocent children to be burnt to death? Tell me.

KONRADIN: He can't control every accident of fate.

HANS: You mean he doesn't care?

KONRADIN: I didn't say that.

HANS: He either doesn't exist – or he exists and is all-powerful, in which case he is monstrous, or he exists and has no power, in which case he is pointless.

KONRADIN: That's too neat.

HANS: Well, what *is* the answer? How can you excuse the burning to death of three children, for God's sake?

KONRADIN: I'm not excusing it! How can you accuse me of excusing it?

HANS: Can't you hear their screams?

KONRADIN: God didn't kill them.

HANS: But he let them die!

They stand.

KONRADIN: But there is good . . . in the world . . .

HANS: I know. But somehow . . .

KONRADIN: What?

HANS: There's no one in charge. There's no one in control. Is there?

Pause.

KONRADIN: There must be.

EXT. A BRIDGE. DAY

HANS *is leaning over the bridge, looking down at the river. Girls in boats float by, laughing.*

KONRADIN *joins him.*

KONRADIN: Hans.

HANS: Hello.

They shake hands.

KONRADIN: How are you?

HANS: All right.

They walk towards a large open-air café.

Hundreds of people. An orchestra playing 'An der Weser'.
Young Nazis at tables. The Nazi salute given in greeting.

KONRADIN: I had a word with my pastor about our talk – about God. I told him what you said. I asked his opinion.

HANS: What was it?

KONRADIN: He said that what you said was blasphemy.

HANS: Do you think it's blasphemy?

KONRADIN: No.

They pass a news kiosk. The VENDOR *offers* KONRADIN *a copy of the* Völkischer Beobachter.

VENDOR: Take it. It's free.

The look at the headlines: 'SHALL GERMANY BE FREE OR A COLONY OF FRANCE?', 'HITLER OR DESTRUCTION'.

KONRADIN: This paper is banned by the government.

He shoves it into a wastebin.
They walk along the terrace. Some Nazis look up at them as they pass.
They sit at a table.

HANS: What do you think of them – the Nazis?

KONRADIN: Not much.

KONRADIN *waves to a waiter.*

I mean, they have no real ideas, do they? They just like dressing up and marching about. Bullies. Just primitive, really.

HANS: What about Hitler?

KONRADIN: Oh, he just rants and raves, doesn't he?

Suddenly at the far end of the terrace a table overturns. SA men jump up, shouting. A man runs along the terrace. They chase him. The man rushes by the boys' table. The boys stand. An SA man collides with HANS. HANS *stands his ground. The SA man pushes him.* KONRADIN *hits the SA man on the jaw. Chaos.*

EXT. A LAKE. DAY

KONRADIN *and* HANS *sitting at the side of the lake with tankards of beer. Their clothes are dishevelled.*
At the other side of the lake, they can discern a procession with banners. Voices sing in the distance.

HANS: I'm frightened.

INT. STRAUSS HOUSE. SITTING-ROOM. EVENING
HANS, *wearing a dinner-jacket, standing, listening to the radio.*
RADIO ANNOUNCER: In the Reichstag elections Hitler has won a
resounding victory. The National Socialist Party has
received 13,750,000 votes. Their seats in Parliament have
increased by 123 – from 107 to 230.
HANS turns the radio off. MOTHER *comes into the room.*
MOTHER: You look so handsome. (*She adjusts his tie.*) Are you
looking forward to it?
HANS: I am. I'm really grateful.
MOTHER: Where's your ticket?
He takes ticket from pocket.
HANS: Here.
He kisses her.
Thank you.

EXT. STUTTGART OPERA HOUSE. NIGHT
Cars and carriages arriving, etc. Posters announcing Fidelio. *Trucks
full of cheering Nazis driving by.* HANS *walking towards the
entrance.*

INT. STUTTGART OPERA HOUSE AUDITORIUM
The orchestra tuning up. HANS *walks to a seat on the aisle midway
down the stalls. He sits. People milling into the auditorium.
Suddenly room is made at the door by the front row of the stalls. The
audience seems to focus on the door. The Lohenburgs make their
entrance.* KONRADIN *comes in first. He is followed by his mother,
the Countess. She is dressed in black with a tiara of diamonds,
diamond necklace and diamond ear-rings. The Count has grey hair
and a grey moustache. A diamond-studded star shines on his jacket.
They stand, receiving bows graciously. At last they move to their
seats.* KONRADIN *greets various people.
The family sits down. The lights go down.*

HANS SITTING IN THE DARK
The opera in action.

THE INTERMISSION
HANS *slipping quickly out of the auditorium. Applause behind him.*

HANS *walks up into the foyer. A great room with marble columns, crystal candelabra, gold-framed mirrors, cyclamen-red carpets, honey-coloured wallpaper.* HANS *leans against one of the columns at the far end of the room. The audience comes in from the auditorium, filling up the foyer.*

The Lohenburg family appears at the other end of the room and begins to walk slowly up its length, nodding to acquaintances. The crowd gives way for them. It is a regal procession.

HANS *waits. They draw nearer.* HANS *stares at the beautiful Countess and then at* KONRADIN. KONRADIN *sees him. He gives no sign of recognition. His eyes flick away. They pass by.*

INT. STRAUSS HOUSE. HANS'S BEDROOM. MORNING

HANS *wakes up suddenly with a gasp. He is sweating. His* FATHER *leans over him.*

FATHER: What is it? What is it? Are you all right?

HANS: Yes, yes. Nothing. I had a nightmare.

FATHER: What nightmare?

HANS: Just a dream. A bad dream.

FATHER *puts his hand on* HANS's *brow.*

FATHER: Hmmnn. Perhaps you should stay at home today.

HANS: No, I'm all right. What's the time?

FATHER: Half-past seven. How was the opera?

HANS: I must get ready.

He jumps out of bed.

EXT. SCHOOL. MORNING

KONRADIN *standing. He sees* HANS *approach.* HANS *walks straight past him and into the school.*

INT. SCHOOLROOM. MORNING

BOLLACHER *standing reciting Latin verbs.* KONRADIN *is looking at* HANS. HANS *avoids his gaze.*

INT. SCHOOL CORRIDOR. MORNING

Bell ringing. Boys milling about. HANS *walking down the corridor.* KONRADIN *calls after him.* HANS *goes on.* KONRADIN *runs down the corridor and catches him up.*

KONRADIN: What's going on? Why aren't you speaking to me?

HANS *does not speak.*

I don't understand.

HANS: You don't understand?

KONRADIN: No.

He stands, breathing hard. HANS *looks at him. They speak in hushed whispers as boys pass up and down the corridor around them.*

HANS: Why did you cut me?

KONRADIN *looks at him.*

KONRADIN: Cut you?

HANS: Yes. Why?

Pause.

Are you ashamed of me?

KONRADIN: No. Not in any way.

HANS: I don't like being humiliated. I refuse to be humiliated.

KONRADIN: It is not my aim . . . to humiliate you. You're my only friend. You know that. You're the only friend I have.

HANS: They why did you cut me?

KONRADIN: I didn't . . . cut you.

HANS: Oh don't be so damn stupid!

KONRADIN *turns away.*

Why have you never introduced me to your parents? You ignored me last night because of them. I know that. I want to know why!

Boys look at them curiously. They are outside the doors of the gym. KONRADIN *looks through the window. The gym is empty.*

KONRADIN: All right. Come in here.

INT. GYM. MORNING

The boys walk into the gym. KONRADIN *closes the door. They walk across the gym to the horizontal bars.*

KONRADIN: I'll tell you why. But you won't like it.

He pauses.

You're a Jew. My mother hates Jews.

They stare at each other.

I didn't *dare* introduce you. She would have insulted you – somehow. My mother comes from a highly . . .

distinguished family. For hundreds of years Jews didn't exist for her people – they were scum of the earth,

84

untouchables. She detests them, she's afraid of them, she has never spoken to a Jew in her life! If she was dying and nobody but your father could save her she wouldn't let him touch her. And she hates you even more because you are my friend. She thinks you've corrupted me, she thinks you're the Devil, a Bolshevik Jewish Devil! (*He laughs, stops.*) I've fought for every hour I've spent with you. I fight her . . . all the time about you!

HANS: And your father?

KONRADIN: My father? Oh, my father has a sense of humour. He calls you 'Little Moses'. He calls me a child.

HANS: I see.

KONRADIN: Anyway, he thinks the Jewish problem is bound to be resolved, sooner or later. He thinks it'll resolve itself.

HANS: How?

KONRADIN: I don't know.

HANS: But what is the Jewish problem, exactly?
    They stare at each other.

KONRADIN: Oh, don't look at me like that! Am I to blame for all this? Am I responsible for my parents? Am I to blame for the world? Why don't you grow up and face the facts? Face reality.
    Pause.
    Look. I should have told you all this before but I'm a coward. I couldn't bear to hurt you. Try to understand.

HANS: (*Slowly*) Yes. You're right. We have to face reality.
    They walk across the gym to the door and go out.

EXT. STUTTGART STREET. EARLY EVENING
HANS *and* KONRADIN *carrying heavy briefcases walking up the hill towards* KONRADIN'*s house. They are silent. They arrive at the gates and stop.*

HANS: It'll be very hot in Sicily, won't it?

KONRADIN: Yes, very hot. But we're quite near the sea. So I shall probably swim every day. What do you think it'll be like in Switzerland?

HANS: Not so hot.
    They stand.

KONRADIN: Let's stay friends. I don't think we should allow –
all this – to spoil our friendship. Do you?

HANS: No.

KONRADIN: So we will go on being friends. Won't we?

HANS: Yes. Yes, of course. Naturally.

> KONRADIN *extends his hand.*

KONRADIN: Have a good holiday.

> *They shake hands.*

HANS: See you in September.

> KONRADIN *opens the gates.* HANS *continues to walk up the hill.*

MONTAGE: SUMMER IN GERMANY 1932

A group of little girls giving the Nazi salute, beaming.
Newsreel in cinema: A parade of Hitler Youth through crowded streets.
A band playing martial music.
Hitler's arrival in Berlin. Vast crowds greeting him.
Couples dancing on an open-air terrace. The song 'I Want a Man, a Real Man'.
Newsreel in cinema: Communist demonstrations against Fascism.
Fires breaking out.
A pretty little girl in white, with flowers, giving Nazi salute.
Newsreel in cinema: Gunfire in the streets.
A Berlin fashion parade.
Newsreel in cinema: Nazi march through working-class district.
Workers running from the police.
Panic in the streets.
Vast torchlight processions.

INT. SCHOOLROOM. DAY

September. The new term. HERR POMPETSKI *walks into the room. He wears a swastika in his buttonhole. He takes his place at the desk. The class is silent.*
HANS *and* KONRADIN *are at their usual places. They look older.*
POMPETSKI: I am your new history master.

> *He looks round the class.*

Gentleman, there is history and history. History which is in
your books now and history which is about to be made.

You know all about the first but you know nothing about
the second because certain dark powers have an interest in
keeping it hidden from you. We'll refer to them as 'dark
powers' for the moment anyway – powers which are at
work everywhere, I am afraid – in Russia, in America and
in our own beloved country. They are an evil destructive
force, intent upon undermining our morals and poisoning
our national heritage. I propose to devote some time in
examining this critical period in our history, which I
personally trust will prove to be a turning of the tide.
The camera closes in on HANS's *face.*
POMPETSKI's *speech goes on, becoming distant and finally*
inaudible.
You have all heard how the Dark Ages followed the fall of
Rome. Do you believe it can have been pure chance that
soon after the German emperors' descent on Italy the
Renaissance began? Or isn't it more than probable that it
was German blood which fertilized the fields of Italy,
barren since the fall of Rome? Can it be a coincidence that
a great civilization was born so soon after the arrival of the
Aryans?

EXT. SCHOOLYARD. DAY
Flag-raising ceremony. The Nazi flag. The majority of masters and
boys giving the Nazi salute. HANS *stands at attention. The ceremony*
ends. The boys mill about. HANS *and* KONRADIN *come face to face.*
HANS: Hello.
KONRADIN: Hello, Hans. How are you?
　　They shake hands warily.
　　How was Switzerland?
HANS: Quite good. Good cheese.
　　They both smile, thinly. The bell rings.

INT. SCHOOL ENTRANCE HALL. DAY
HANS *comes in.* BOLLACHER, ERHARDT *and some others turn and*
look at him.
ERHARDT *holds his nose. The others grin.* BOLLACHER *calls.*
BOLLACHER: Strauss! Wait a minute!
　　HANS *stops, turns.*

87

KONRADIN *comes into the hall and stops, watching.*
BOLLACHER *walks up to* HANS. *He holds a sticker. He lifts it up to* HANS's *face.*
Read this.

HANS: Take it away. Take it away from my face.

BOLLACHER: Read it. Read it aloud!
They stare at each other.
All right. I will. (*He reads.*) 'The Jews have ruined Germany. German people – awake!'
KONRADIN *takes a step towards* BOLLACHER.

KONRADIN: Bollacher –
BOLLACHER *turns, looks sharply at* KONRADIN. KONRADIN *stops.*
BOLLACHER *moves closer to* HANS. *He sticks the sticker on to Hans's jacket.*

BOLLACHER: Why don't you go back to Palestine where you came from? Jew boy.
HANS *hits him. They fight.* KONRADIN *watches.* BOLLACHER *falls, hits his head.* POMPETSKI *comes down the main stairs.*

POMPETSKI: What's this?

BOLLACHER: Sir! He attacked me!

POMPETSKI: (*To* HANS) Did you attack him?

HANS: Yes.

POMPETSKI: Why?

HANS: He insulted me.

POMPETSKI: Oh, really? What did he say?

HANS: He told me to go back to Palestine.

POMPETSKI: But that's not an insult, Strauss. It's sound, friendly advice. (*To* BOLLACHER) Be patient. Now all of you get back to your classrooms. We will have order in this country and I shall have order in this school.

EXT. STREET. DAY
HANS *walking up the hill by himself.*

EXT. STRAUSS HOUSE. DAY
HANS *approaching his house. He stops.*
A Nazi is standing outside the house with a large poster: 'Germans! Avoid all Jews. Whoever has anything to do with a Jew is defiled.'

FATHER *comes out of the house dressed in officer's uniform with decorations including Iron Cross first class. He holds an officer's sword. He stands to attention beside the Nazi.* MOTHER *can be seen through a curtain at the window.*

A crowd gathers. It begins to mutter. Low jeers directed at the Nazi. A Nazi truck arrives. Jeers and catcalls from the truck. The Nazi rolls up the poster and climbs into the truck. The truck drives away. The crowds drifts away.

HANS *walks slowly to the house. He stops in front of his* FATHER. FATHER *looks at him, takes him by the arm and leads him into the house.*

INT. STRAUSS HOUSE. SITTING-ROOM. DAY

FATHER, MOTHER, HANS.

FATHER: (*To* HANS) Sit down.

> *He does.*
> We have something to say to you which we know will be a shock to you, but it must be said and it must be done.
> *Pause.*
> Your mother and I have decided to send you to America, for the time being anyway, until the storm has blown over. You will stay with your uncle in New York. He'll look after you and arrange for you to go to university. You can't go to a university here. You know that. You're not a fool.
> *Pause.*
> We are staying here. We intend to join you . . . later. Please accept this. Please don't speak.
> *Pause.*
> I have booked you on the *Bremen* which sails on October 5th.

INT. SCHOOLROOM. DAY

HANS *clearing his desk, putting papers and books into a briefcase. Other boys lounging about.*

BOLLACHER *and* ERHARDT *stand by the window singing softly.*

BOLLACHER *and* ERHARDT: Little yid – we bid you farewell
> May you join Moses and Isaac in hell

Little yid – never come back,
or we'll break your filthy, lousy neck.

HANS *leaves the room.*

EXT. STREET. EVENING

HANS *walking up the hill.* KONRADIN *steps out of a doorway.*
HANS *stops.* KONRADIN *comes towards him.*

KONRADIN: When are you going?

HANS: Tomorrow.

Pause.

KONRADIN: I'm sorry it's come to this. But it probably makes
sense – just for the time being. The country will be in a
state of flux for a while, I should think. But the fact is we
want a new Germany and we're going to get it.

HANS *looks at him, expressionless.*

Listen . . . I want to tell you . . . I believe in Hitler. I met
him in Munich recently. He really impressed me. He's . . .
totally sincere, you see. He has such . . . he has true
passion. I think that he can save our country. He's our only
hope.

HANS *stands staring at him.*

Look. I'm sure that in a couple of years you'll be able to
come back. Germany needs people like you. I'm sure that
the Führer will be willing to choose between the good
Jewish elements and the . . . undesirable Jewish elements.

Pause.

I've learnt so much from you, you know. You've taught me
to think. You have. Truly.

He extends his hand.

Good luck.

HANS *does not take his hand. They stand still.* HANS *turns
away and runs up the hill.* KONRADIN *opens the gates and goes
in.*

EXT. NEW YORK PIER. WINTER. DAY

HANS *walking on to the pier. He is greeted by his uncle. His uncle
embraces him. He then takes him by the arm and walks along the
pier with him, talking quietly.*

INT. STRAUSS HOUSE. NIGHT
FATHER *closing all windows.*
He goes into the kitchen, turns on the gas.
He goes up to the bedroom.

INT. STRAUSS HOUSE. BEDROOM. NIGHT
FATHER *gets into bed, holds his sleeping wife.*

INT. STRAUSS HOUSE. KITCHEN. NIGHT
The hissing gas.

INT. COURTROOM. DAY
Black and white. JUDGE FREISLER *screaming at* ALEX (*Henry's
granddaughter*), *who stands in the dock wide-eyed. Cut to* LISA
(*Henry's daughter*) *lying on the floor between two pairs of jackboots,
her hand stretched out, sobbing.*

INT. HOTEL BEDROOM. PRESENT. NIGHT
HENRY *wakes up sweating.*

INT. HOTEL. DAY
HENRY *at reception desk.*
HENRY: I would like to stay for a few more days. Is that all
    right?
RECEPTIONIST: How many days would that be?
HENRY: Oh . . . three or four. Perhaps five.
RECEPTIONIST: Yes, that will be fine.
HENRY: Will you cancel my flight?
RECEPTIONIST: Of course.

EXT. KONRADIN'S HOUSE. DAY
*Taxi drives in through the gate, under the arch and up the winding
road to the villa.*
HENRY *gets out and goes into the house.*

INT. KONRADIN'S HOUSE. DAY
HENRY *stands for a moment in the hall and looks about. The
architecture has not altered but the hall is completely bare. A coat
rack along the wall.*

Four GIRLS *descend the stairs. They look at him.*

HENRY: Excuse me . . . does anyone speak English?

GIRL: Yes.

HENRY: What is this house now?

GIRL: This house?

HENRY: Yes. What . . . happens here?

GIRL: This is a special house for income taxes. Special income taxes department of Stuttgart.

HENRY: Oh.

GIRL: Can I help you?

HENRY: I would like information about a family who lived here. Called Lohenburg. Before the war.

GIRL: Taxes information?

HENRY: No, no. Just . . . what happened to them?

GIRL: I do not know them.

HENRY: Is there anyone . . . ?

GIRL: (*Shrugs and points up the stairs.*) Up there, perhaps.

HENRY: Thank you.

> *The* GIRLS *go out.*
> HENRY *walks up the stairs and comes face to face with the doors of mother's bedroom. The doors have not been changed.* HENRY *opens the door and looks in.*

INT. ROOM. DAY

The room is bare. A long oval table. Chairs.
A large television screen. HENRY *stands still, looking at the room.*
Suddenly an inner door opens. A MAN *appears, stops abruptly.*

MAN: (*In German*) Can I help you?

HENRY: I'm sorry, I . . . Before the war a family called Lohenburg lived here. I wonder if you have –
The MAN *interrupts him politely, shrugging.*

MAN: (*In German*) I'm so sorry, I speak no English. (*He mutters*) Lohenburg? Yes . . . yes. (*He smiles and speaks in English.*) Our Director . . . of this place . . . is here . . . what is it? . . . not today . . . ?

HENRY: Tomorrow?

MAN: Yes, yes. Tomorrow. He knows . . . this house, the history . . .

HENRY: Tomorrow. I'll be back.

MAN: Lohenburg . . . ja . . .

> HENRY *looks at him expectantly. The* MAN *goes to the door, opens it wide, bows.*

Tomorrow . . . yes?

> HENRY *steps on to the landing. The* MAN *closes the door.*

EXT. COUNTRY ROAD. DAY

A taxi approaches the gates of a large estate. It goes through the gates and drives up to the house. HENRY *gets out of the taxi. He climbs the steps to the front door, rings the bell and waits. A* SERVANT *opens the door.*

SERVANT: Guten Morgen.

HENRY: Good morning. Can you tell me – if the von Zeilarn family is still in residence here?

SERVANT: (*In German*) This is the home of the Gräfin von Zeilarn und Lizen, yes.

HENRY: Is the Gräfin – by any chance – here?

> *Pause.*

SERVANT: She is at home, yes.

HENRY: Will you give her my card?

> *He gives the* SERVANT *the card. The* SERVANT *withdraws.* HENRY *turns and looks out at the grounds.*
> *The* SERVANT *returns.*

SERVANT: This way please.

INT. ZEILARN HOUSE. DAY

The SERVANT *leads* HENRY *into the drawing-room.*
The GRÄFIN *is a tall woman in her early seventies. She stands erect.*

HENRY: Thank you so much for seeing me.

GRÄFIN: (*Looking at card*) I don't recall our meeting.

HENRY: It was many years ago.

GRÄFIN: But you are American.

HENRY: Yes.

GRÄFIN: Did we meet in America?

HENRY: No, no. Here. In this house.

> *She frowns.*

GRÄFIN: In this house? Please sit down.

> *They sit.*

HENRY: I was brought to see you by Konradin von Lohenburg.

GRÄFIN: By whom?

HENRY: Konradin von Lohenburg.

> *She stares at him.*

Your cousin.

GRÄFIN: When was this?

HENRY: In 1932.

> *The* GRÄFIN *glances out of the window.*

GRÄFIN: Wonderful days.

> *She looks back at him.*

I remember no such meeting.

HENRY: I am not in the least surprised. I was a young boy of no
. . . consequence. It is a very long time ago.

GRÄFIN: But what were you doing in Germany . . . in 1932?

HENRY: I lived here, with my family, in Stuttgart.

GRÄFIN: You said you were an American.

HENRY: I have become an American. I left Germany in 1932.

GRÄFIN: Why?

HENRY: I am Jewish.

> *Silence. The* GRÄFIN *is expressionless.*

This is my first visit to Germany . . . for fifty-five years.

GRÄFIN: And what can I do for you?

> *Pause.*

HENRY: I was a close friend of Konradin von Lohenburg.

GRÄFIN: Were you?

HENRY: I don't know what happened to him. I would like to
know what happened to him. Did he survive the war? Do
you know . . . Madame? Can you tell me?

> *She stands.*

GRÄFIN: It is not a subject I am willing to discuss. I trust you
will find your visit to Germany of interest. Please excuse
me.

> *She inclines her head and leaves the room.*
> *He remains standing.*

INT. STUTTGART STATE ART GALLERY. DAY

An exhibition of the photographs of John Copelans. HENRY
walking through the gallery, looking at them.

Over this a general rumble of passing people: murmurs and snatches

*of conversation in many languages. Bursts of laughter from
schoolchildren.*
HENRY *walks through the crowd and into the lobby. His eye drifts
over the posters and postcard counter. He suddenly stiffens. He
walks to a poster and bends down to examine it. It is an
announcement of an art exhibition at the Karl Alexander
Gymnasium. He stares at it.*

EXT. STREET TAXI RANK. DAY
HENRY *getting into taxi. The* TAXI DRIVER *is a man in his sixties.*

INT. TAXI. DAY
HENRY: Hotel Am Schlossgarten.
    The taxi drives off.
    Suddenly HENRY *leans forward, taps the* DRIVER *on the
    shoulder, points to a street.*
    Up there.
TAXI DRIVER: Hotel Schlossgarten?
HENRY: No, no. Up there!
    The DRIVER *shrugs and turns left.*

EXT. STREET. DAY
The taxi driving uphill towards the Strauss house.

INT. TAXI. DAY
HENRY: Stop.
    The taxi stops. Henry sits staring at the house. The TAXI
    DRIVER *looks at his watch and clicks his teeth.*
    (*Quietly*) That was my house. My parents died there. You
    understand?
    The TAXI DRIVER *turns his head.*
TAXI DRIVER: (*In German*) What?
HENRY: Do you understand?
TAXI DRIVER: Nein.
HENRY: My parents died there. They killed themselves there.
TAXI DRIVER: (*In German*) I don't understand.
HENRY: My father fought for Germany. But he was a Jew. They
    died of despair. Do you understand?

TAXI DRIVER: Nein.

HENRY: What do you mean? What do you mean, nein?
(*Savagely, in German*) What do you mean, nein? Of course
you understand! You understand perfectly well! He was
Jewish! You understand that perfectly well! You bastard!

TAXI DRIVER: (*In German*) You get out.
He opens Henry's door. HENRY *gets out.*

EXT. STREET. DAY
The taxi drives away. HENRY *stands still for a moment. He walks
away down the hill.*

INT. PEOPLE'S COURT, BERLIN (1944). DAY
Black and white.
JUDGE FREISLER *enters the courtroom. The court rises.* FREISLER
gives the Nazi salute and sits.

INT. CEMETERY: OFFICE. DAY
HENRY *walks into the office. A* MAN *looks up from a table.*

MAN: (*In German*) Yes?

HENRY: (*In German*) I believe there are some Jewish graves in
this cemetery.

MAN: Jewish? Some. Yes.

HENRY: I would like to look at them, please.
The MAN *leads* HENRY *to the door. They go out.*

EXT. CEMETERY. DAY
The MAN *points to a far corner of the cemetery.*

MAN: Some Jews over there. Behind the trees.

HENRY: Thank you.
HENRY *begins to walk towards the trees.*

INT. PEOPLE'S COURT, BERLIN (1944)
Black and white.
A man stands before FREISLER. *He is unshaven, wears an open-
necked shirt, is holding his trousers up. He is heavily set, in his
fifties.*

FREISLER: (*In German*) The German people spit on you. You

are standing in the People's Court of Germany and the German people spit on you.

EXT. CEMETERY. DAY
HENRY *arrives at the Jewish graves. He examines them. They are overgrown, almost buried.*
He bends to one, pulls twigs and leaves away from it. He finally discerns a faint inscription: 'Captain and Frau Strauss May 1934'. He stands upright and remains looking down.

INT. PEOPLE'S COURT, BERLIN (1944)
Black and white.
Another MAN *stands in front of* FREISLER. *He is short, in his forties.*
FREISLER: Are you *proud* of his act? Do I hear *pride* in your voice?
MAN: I don't see –
FREISLER: Answer the question!
MAN: We had good reasons –
FREISLER: Good reasons! You stinking traitor! Your soul runs with pus! You have broken your oath not once but twice! You are a criminal hypocrite and a filthy liar! The Reich knows what to do with vermin like you!

EXT. SCHOOL. DAY
Milling students. HENRY *walking towards the school.*

INT. SCHOOL. HEADMASTER'S OFFICE. DAY
BROSSNER, *a man in his forties, casually dressed.*
BROSSNER: Herr Strauss. Hello. How are you?
They shake hands.
HENRY: We spoke on the telephone.
BROSSNER: Yes, yes. I know. Sit down. (*He laughs.*) It isn't often I meet 'old boys' from so long ago. In fact I'm not sure I ever have.
HENRY: (*Looking around*) But this . . . isn't the same school.
BROSSNER: It was totally destroyed.
HENRY: No, I meant . . . you have girls here now . . . for example.

BROSSNER: Oh, yes. Of course.

> *Pause.*

You haven't been in this country at all . . . since then?

HENRY: No. Not since I was a boy. I've had no contact with Germany at all, in fact, until now. I haven't read a German book or a German newspaper. I haven't spoken a word of the German language . . . in all that time.

> BROSSNER *grunts.*

BROSSNER: You wanted to know about the class of '32. Many died in the war. We collected information about them . . . about all the dead . . . over the years. It's in this book.

> *He shows* HENRY *a book with a plain soft cover.*

But we also have a war memorial. Would you like to see it?

> HENRY *is silent for a moment.*

HENRY: Yes.

EXT. SCHOOL TERRACE. DAY

A group of tall schoolboys kicking a ball about. BROSSNER, *holding the book, brings* HENRY *through glass doors on to the terrace and points to a wall.*

Attached to the wall a large war memorial, containing over one hundred names.

HENRY *stands, looking at it.*

HENRY: How did Bollacher die? Is it known?

> BROSSNER *looks in the book.*

BROSSNER: Bollacher . . . on the Russian front.

HENRY: And Erhardt?

BROSSNER: Erhardt . . . shot down – over London.

> HENRY *looks at the list of names beginning with L. There he sees 'Konradin von Lohenburg'.*
>
> *He turns to* BROSSNER.

HENRY: And Lohenburg?

> BROSSNER *stares at him.*

BROSSNER: Lohenburg?

INT. EMPTY EXECUTION ROOM. DAY

The room is bare. Two windows at the back. Winter sunshine slanting in. A rafter along the ceiling in front of the window. Butcher's hooks hanging down.

Over this BROSSNER's *voice.*

BROSSNER: (*Voice over*) You don't know? He was implicated in
  the plot against Hitler. Executed.
  The butcher's hooks glint in the light from the window.

Turtle Diary

Turtle Diary was produced in 1985. The cast was as follows:

NEAERA DUNCAN	Glenda Jackson
WILLIAM SNOW	Ben Kingsley
JOHNSON	Richard Johnson
GEORGE FAIRBAIRN	Michael Gambon
MRS INCHCLIFF	Rosemary Leach
MISS NEAP	Eleanor Bron
HARRIET SIMS	Harriet Walter
SANDOR	Jeroen Krabbe
PUBLISHER	Nigel Hawthorne
MR MEAGER	Michael Aldridge
LORRY DRIVER	Gary Olsen
MAN IN BOOKSHOP	Harold Pinter
Director	John Irvin
Producer	Richard Johnson
Production Designer	Leo Austin
Photography	Peter Hannan
Costume Designer	Elizabeth Waller
Editor	Peter Tanner
Composer	Geoffrey Burgon

GIANT TURTLES SWIMMING IN THE SEA
They are swimming towards a tropical beach. Brilliant sunlight.
Camera pulls back to reveal that the film is on a video display in an
aquarium.
Camera pans to turtles in a tank. Soaring, dipping and curving.
They loop away and then swing towards the glass.
Camera pans to find WILLIAM, *looking at turtles. Black silhouettes*
of people holding children up to the glass.
Echoing footsteps, cries of children, running.

THE TURTLES

WILLIAM
He turns, walks away through the people. He passes NEAERA. *The*
camera stays with her. She is watching the turtles.

INT. AQUARIUM
WILLIAM *passing green windows.*
Glimpses of crab, lobster, tropical fish, toads, newts, etc.
Door of aquarium slams, echoes.

INT. BLOOMSBURY BOOKSHOP. DAY
HARRIET (*twenty-three*) *on short stepladder reaching for a book.*
WILLIAM *at table handing wrapped book to a man.*
WILLIAM: Thank you very much, sir.
> HARRIET *descends ladder.* WILLIAM *turns. Her bottom bumps*
> *into him.*
HARRIET: (*Giggling*) Sorry.
WILLIAM: Sorry for what?
> *A* WOMAN *approaches* MR MEAGER (*elderly*).
WOMAN: There's a new book just come out. Could you . . . ?
> Historical. Terribly well reviewed. Do you know what it is?
MR MEAGER: Er . . . let me see . . . I wonder . . .
> *He looks at* WILLIAM.
WILLIAM: Might it be . . . *Servant to the King* by Jean Bright?

WOMAN: That's it. How clever.

WILLIAM: Yes, that's it. Going like a bomb with the menopausal set.

WOMAN: What did you say?

WILLIAM: Going like a bomb, it's the best she's written yet.
WOMAN *looks at him dubiously*. MR MEAGER *coughs*.

INT. PUBLISHER'S OFFICE. DAY
PUBLISHER *kissing* NEAERA's *cheek at reception area. They walk through open-plan office.*

PUBLISHER: Lovely to see you. How are you?

NEAERA: Oh, fine.

PUBLISHER: You look wonderful.

NEAERA: Oh . . .
She laughs.

PUBLISHER: Come and have a drink.
He opens the door to his office. They go in.
What will you have?
On the wall is a poster for Gillian Vole's Jumble Sale. *He points to it.*
The success of the sales conference!

NEAERA: Really?

PUBLISHER: Sherry? Gin? Vodka?
Enter SECOND PUBLISHER.

SECOND PUBLISHER: Neaera! Hello!

NEAERA: Hello.

SECOND PUBLISHER: See the poster?

NEAERA: Yes.

SECOND PUBLISHER: The success of the sales conference.

PUBLISHER: Sherry? Gin? Vodka?

SECOND PUBLISHER: Gin.

PUBLISHER: Not you.

NEAERA: Vodka. Why not?

PUBLISHER: Why not indeed! (*To* SECOND PUBLISHER) What about you? (*To* NEAERA) I think it's going to do even better than *Gillian Vole's Christmas.*
He gives her vodka.
Cheers. I'll have . . . let's see . . . what will I have?

SECOND PUBLISHER: Gin.

PUBLISHER: I hate gin.
SECOND PUBLISHER: No, I'd like one.
PUBLISHER: Yes, I know that. But what about me?
SECOND PUBLISHER: (*To* NEAERA) What's next?
NEAERA: Oh . . . God . . . I don't know.
PUBLISHER: (*To* NEAERA) I'll join you in a vodka. Why not?
NEAERA: Why not indeed?
PUBLISHER: What little animal have you got up your sleeve
     now?
NEAERA: What about a water beetle?
PUBLISHER: A water beetle! How lovely. (*He pours.*) What
     is it?
SECOND PUBLISHER: Shall I help myself?
NEAERA: Cheers.
PUBLISHER: Cheers.
     SECOND PUBLISHER *pours a drink.*
NEAERA: Well, it's just a beetle which lives in the water.
SECOND PUBLISHER: (*Muttering*) Promising.
NEAERA: Actually . . .
PUBLISHER: Mmnn?
NEAERA: Actually . . . I think I might have come to the end.
SECOND PUBLISHER: What do you mean?
NEAERA: I can't draw. I can't write.
PUBLISHER: Don't be silly.
SECOND PUBLISHER: A temporary condition.
PUBLISHER: Have another vodka.

EXT. PARSONS GREEN. THE COMMON. EVENING
*An Underground train, above ground, passing the Common on its
way to Putney Bridge.*
*The lights of the train. It slows down. Signals go from red to green.
The train moves.*

EXT. STREET. EVENING
*Lamplight. Woman walking with greyhound. Man, dragging one
leg, walking behind.*

EXT. WILLIAM'S HOUSE. EVENING
Lighted window on the ground floor. MRS INCHCLIFF *glimpsed*

through furniture. She is bending over a sideboard using an electric sander.
Camera pans to upper window. WILLIAM *looking out.*

INT. WILLIAM'S HOUSE. WILLIAM'S ROOM. EVENING
WILLIAM *staring out of the window.*

WILLIAM'S POINT OF VIEW
Couple with greyhound in the distance. Another train passes, going fast.
Shouts. Youths run into the children's playground. They jump on to the swings, swing violently.

INT. WILLIAM'S HOUSE. BATHROOM. NIGHT
Bath-water running out. Hair in bath. Scum.
SANDOR's *bare legs leaving bathroom. He goes on to the landing.*

INT. WILLIAM'S HOUSE. LANDING. MORNING
In a corner of the landing a cooker, fridge and sink.
SANDOR *is heavy-set, moustached. He goes to the cooker, shovels food from a saucepan on to a plate. Some of the food spills on to the cooker. He turns off the gas, goes to his room, slams the door.*
WILLIAM *comes out of his room, goes to the cooker, sees mess, grimaces, looks viciously towards Sandor's door. He takes rag, wipes cooker.*

EXT. STREET. DAY
NEAERA *wheeling a pushchair. On the pushchair a small tank and aquarium gear. She walks towards a large house in a square.*

INT. NEAERA'S HOUSE
The house consists of self-contained flats.
She pulls the pushchair up the stairs, arrives at her landing. A flat door opens. JOHNSON *comes out. He wears a three-piece dark suit, carries a briefcase and overnight bag.*
JOHNSON: Hello. What's that? Setting up an aquarium?
NEAERA: Yes.
JOHNSON: Really? How funny. I've had one for years.
NEAERA: Have you?

106

JOHNSON: Yes, I've been keeping fish for years. Black Mollies.
　　Nothing flash. What are you going to put in yours?
NEAERA: I thought . . . a water beetle.
JOHNSON: Fascinating. Should make a fascinating pet. Any time
　　you'd like some snails, let me know. I've got tons of them.
　　She stares at him.
　　They keep the tank clean, you see.
NEAERA: Oh. Well, thank you.
JOHNSON: I'd give you a hand setting that thing up, but I'm on
　　my way to Heathrow.
NEAERA: Going somewhere nice?
JOHNSON: Oh, Amsterdam, Vienna. That sort of thing. Good
　　luck with the beetle.

EXT. THE COMMON. NIGHT
MISS NEAP *walking towards the house. She holds a theatre
programme in her hand. She sees a light in the front window. Stops.*

INT. WILLIAM'S HOUSE. MRS INCHCLIFF'S WORKROOM.
NIGHT
*The room is crammed with furniture and objects, pieces of wood. A
workbench.* MRS INCHCLIFF *sitting at it under a green-shaded light,
planing a piece of wood. She wears jeans, shirt and sandals.*
WILLIAM *sits by her with a cup of tea.*
MRS INCHCLIFF: Have you ever done any of this?
WILLIAM: Oh . . . once. Yes. A bit of it. When I had a house. I
　　used to make things for my girls.
MRS INCHCLIFF: What things?
WILLIAM: Oh . . . you know . . . this and that.

INT. FRONT DOOR
MISS NEAP *closing the door. She goes towards the room, hears
voices, stops.*

INT. WORKROOM
MRS INCHCLIFF: Did you make things for your wife, too?
WILLIAM: (*Laughing*) My wife? No.
MRS INCHCLIFF: (*Calling*) Hello!

107

WILLIAM *turns to see* MISS NEAP *hovering in the shadows of the hall. She comes forward into the doorway.*

WILLIAM: Hello, Miss Neap.

MISS NEAP: Oh, hello.

MRS INCHCLIFF: Cup of tea?

MISS NEAP: Oh, no. No, thank you. I have to go to Leeds to see my mother in the morning.

WILLIAM: Do you come from Leeds?

MISS NEAP: Me? Oh yes. I do.

MRS INCHCLIFF: How is your mother?

MISS NEAP: Oh . . . she's quite old now.

WILLIAM: Been to the theatre?

MISS NEAP: Oh . . . yes.

WILLIAM: Good?

MISS NEAP: Mmnn.

WILLIAM: What was it?

MISS NEAP: Umm . . . well, it was a farce.

WILLIAM: Ah.

MRS INCHCLIFF: (*To* WILLIAM) You should go up to the theatre some time. See a bit of life. Young man like you.

WILLIAM *laughs shortly.*

MISS NEAP: Well . . .

She smiles briefly, stands uncertainly.

EXT. THE SQUARE. NIGHT. 3 A.M.
Long shot. A figure sitting on a bench, alone. Orange sky. London hum.

EXT. THE SQUARE. NIGHT. 3 A.M.
Close shot. NEAERA *on the bench.*

THE TURTLES
They swoop in the tank, their flippers click against the glass as they turn.

VOICE: The Green Sea Turtle, *Chelonia Mydas*, is the source of turtle soup.

INT. AQUARIUM
A boy listening to a recorded guide. In background, WILLIAM
listening.
VOICE: The Green Turtle swims 1,400 miles to breed and lay
    eggs on Ascension Island in the South Atlantic, halfway to
    Africa. Ascension Island is only five miles long – nobody
    knows how they find it.

INT. AQUARIUM
WILLIAM *walks away towards the exit.*

EXT. AQUARIUM. DAY
WILLIAM *comes out. He bumps into* NEAERA, *who is walking
towards the entrance.*
WILLIAM: Sorry.
    They look at each other.
NEAERA: Sorry.
    She goes in.

INT. AQUARIUM
NEAERA *stands by the turtle tank. At the far end of the aquarium*
GEORGE *(head keeper) standing among a group of children. They
are asking questions. Words indecipherable. Echoes.*
*She moves towards the group, stops, hovers. The children run
towards the exit.* GEORGE *walks away. Tentatively, she approaches
him.*
NEAERA: Excuse me.
GEORGE: Morning.
NEAERA: These turtles . . . how long have they been here?
GEORGE: The big ones? The big ones have been here about
    thirty years.
    She looks at them, and then at him.
NEAERA: That's a very long time.
GEORGE: It is.
NEAERA: Are they happy?
    He laughs.
GEORGE: Happy? No, I wouldn't think they're all that happy.
    Born for the ocean, you see.
NEAERA: Yes.

They stand.
Thank you.

INT. NEAERA'S FLAT. DAY
The water beetle. It is lying on damp moss.
Voices of children from the street.
NEAERA *prods the beetle with a pencil into a little net, lifts the aquarium cover, lets the beetle into the water. The beetle swims down to a plastic 'shipwreck'.* NEAERA *watches it, and then looks about her room.*
The room is bright. A work table. A drawing board, etc. A number of illustrations on the wall, of children's books. Volumes of the books on shelves.
She picks up a china figure of a 1900 bathing beauty sitting on a turtle. She turns the figure to face the tank.

INT. BOOKSHOP. OFFICE. DAY
WILLIAM *with coffee.*
MR MEAGER *comes in, pours coffee.*
MR MEAGER: Had bad news yesterday.
WILLIAM: What?
MR MEAGER: Penrose died.
WILLIAM: Penrose?
MR MEAGER: Yes, just like that.
WILLIAM: What . . . you mean old . . .?
MR MEAGER: Old Penrose. Yes. He wasn't all that old, either.
    Through the office window, WILLIAM *sees* NEAERA *enter the shop. He stands.*
WILLIAM: Dear dear.
    He goes into the shop.

INT. BOOKSHOP
NEAERA *picks up a large book on turtles from a table and opens it.*
WILLIAM *joins* HARRIET.
HARRIET: What are you doing this weekend?
WILLIAM: Me? Oh . . . nothing much. What about you?
HARRIET: I'm going to the country. Friends. Lovely house. In the Chilterns.
WILLIAM: Ah.

HARRIET: Do you like the country?
  He looks at her blankly.
WILLIAM: What?
HARRIET: Do you like the country?
WILLIAM: The country. Yes. I used to, yes.
HARRIET: Used to? Well, what do you like now?
  A customer approaches. She moves away. He looks across to
  NEAERA, *who is still reading the book. She closes it, goes to*
  him.
NEAERA: I'd like this, please.
WILLIAM: Certainly.
  He looks at the book. A large turtle on the cover. He wraps the
  book. NEAERA *puts cash on the table.*
NEAERA: Have you anything else on sea turtles, apart from this?
WILLIAM: No. I don't think so, nothing else. We've got Carr, of
  course. Have you read Carr?
  She looks directly at him, recognizes him.
NEAERA: Yes, I have.
WILLIAM: Oh, you have? Good book, isn't it?
NEAERA: Wonderful.
WILLIAM: Yes. Well, this one's pretty interesting too. It's –
  A MAN *approaches, book in hand.*
MAN: Have you got the sequel to this?
WILLIAM: Sequel? Is there one?
MAN: Somebody told me there was one.
NEAERA: Thank you.
  NEAERA *leaves the shop.* WILLIAM *glances at her and then*
  looks at the book.
WILLIAM: No, this is the sequel to the one before, you see.
MAN: The one before?

EXT. ZOO. DAY
WILLIAM *walking through the Zoo.*

INT. AQUARIUM
GEORGE *cleaning tank windows. The suds run down the glass.*
Suddenly reflected through the suds: WILLIAM. *He is standing still,*
looking at GEORGE. GEORGE *turns.*
GEORGE: Afternoon.

III

WILLIAM: Good afternoon. I just wondered . . . these
    turtles . . .

GEORGE: Yes?

WILLIAM: Any chance of looking at them . . . from the other
    side?

GEORGE: Why do you want to do that?

WILLIAM: Oh . . . curiosity.

GEORGE: I'll just finish this job. All right?

WILLIAM: Yes. Yes, of course.

    GEORGE *cleans the window.* WILLIAM *stands.*

TURTLES THROUGH THE SUDS.

INT. HEAD KEEPER'S ROOM

GEORGE *leads* WILLIAM *through the room, on to planks across the
back of the tank. They look down at the turtles.*

GEORGE: That's not the colour they'd be in natural light. The
    colour fades here.

WILLIAM: Not too big a space for them, is it?

GEORGE: Not too big, no.

WILLIAM: Do you ever move them out?

GEORGE: When we clean the tank, yes. We put them in the
    filters.

WILLIAM: Is that difficult?

GEORGE: Bit awkward getting them through the hole, you have
    to mind their jaws. But it's not too difficult.

WILLIAM: Ah.

    Pause.

    Tell me, suppose some turtle freak decided to steal these
    turtles. What would he need for the job?

    GEORGE *begins to roll a cigarette.*

GEORGE: What would he want to do with them – after he'd
    stolen them?

WILLIAM: Put them back in the sea.

GEORGE: Ah. Well, he'd need a trolley to get them out of here,
    and crates to put them in, and a van to take them down to
    the ocean.

WILLIAM: Wouldn't they dry out – on the trip?

GEORGE: Funny. You're the second person this week who's

asked me about the turtles. No, drying out's no problem.
Put them on wet sacks, you see. Throw a bucket at them
every now and again. They'd be all right.

WILLIAM: A bucket?

GEORGE: Yes. To wet them down.

WILLIAM: But what about the Channel? Wouldn't it be too cold
for them?

GEORGE: Cold water makes them a little sluggish but I think
they'd backtrack up the North Atlantic current till they hit
the Canary current or the Gulf Stream. They'd be in home
waters in three months.

WILLIAM: Mmnn. Who was the other person?

GEORGE: Eh?

WILLIAM: Who was the other person – who asked you about the
turtles?

GEORGE: A lady.

WILLIAM: Ah. Oh yes. Well, I might give you a ring some time.

GEORGE: Any time.

    WILLIAM *takes out notebook.*

    George Fairbairn. Head Keeper. 722 2180.

WILLIAM: Thanks.

INT. WILLIAM'S ROOM. NIGHT
WILLIAM *in bed, smoking. Shouts of youths passing the house.*
Mock groans and screams.

EXT. THE COMMON. NIGHT
A tube train in the distance, coming closer.

EXT. PLAYGROUND. NIGHT
A swing sent up violently, tangled.

WILLIAM IN BED, EYES OPEN

INT. LANDING. NIGHT
SANDOR *shovelling food on to a plate. Cooker spattered. Slam of*
door.

THE WATER BEETLE. NIGHT
The beetle swimming in the tank. NEAERA's *legs moving past the tank. The bathing beauty and the turtle.* NEAERA *stands by the window, looking out. Her back.*

EXT. FESTIVAL HALL. DAY
People sitting on benches, reading the Sunday newspapers. NEAERA *comes into shot. She looks up at Hungerford Bridge. A train is passing.*

EXT. TRAIN ON HUNGERFORD BRIDGE
The sky is framed in each window as the carriages pass. Rectangles of blue. The train passes. Blue sky.

NEAERA'S FACE

EXT. THE SQUARE. DAY
NEAERA *approaches her house.*
A car draws up. A chauffeur gets out, opens the back door.
JOHNSON *gets out, with a briefcase. Chauffeur gives him a suitcase.*
JOHNSON *sees* NEAERA. *The car drives away. He waits for her. She crosses the road.*
JOHNSON: Hello. How's the beetle?
NEAERA: Quite well, I think.
JOHNSON: Must pop in and see it some time. Trouble is, I'm
    always rushing about. No rest for the wicked.
NEAERA: Where've you been this time?
JOHNSON: Oh, Bahrain, Abu Dhabi . . . you know, that kind of
    thing.

INT. NEAERA'S HOUSE. STAIRS
NEAERA *and* JOHNSON *ascending.*
NEAERA: What do you do, exactly?
    He laughs, puts fingers to lips.
JOHNSON: Top secret. God, I hate travelling. Well, love to your
    beetle. (*He opens the door to his flat, turns.*) Oh, what is it,
    by the way, male or female?
NEAERA: Female. There were no males available.

INT. WILLIAM'S HOUSE. BATHROOM
Scum in bath. Hairs. WILLIAM, *gritting teeth, cleans the bath.*

NEAERA'S TANK
NEAERA *is kneeling by the tank. The beetle swims.*
Through the water in the tank, through the window, glimpses of
rooftop and sky.

EXT. REGENT'S PARK. DAY
Brilliant sun. People with ice-creams and soft drinks, rowing boats
on the lake. A band playing. Children.
The Zoo in the distance.
WILLIAM *walking towards the Zoo. His face set.*

INT. AQUARIUM. HEAD KEEPER'S ROOM. DAY
GEORGE: What do you think of this?
    He hands WILLIAM *a black baby turtle, nine inches long.*
    WILLIAM *holds it. It waggles its flippers.*
WILLIAM: Friendly.
GEORGE: They are.
    GEORGE *takes it, puts it in a small tank.*
WILLIAM: Tell me . . .
GEORGE: Yes?
WILLIAM: What if this turtle freak . . . were to seriously
    propose a turtle theft . . . to the Head Keeper?
GEORGE: You mean me?
WILLIAM: You. Yes.
GEORGE: And you're the freak?
WILLIAM: I am. Yes.
GEORGE: I'd be with you all the way. Have a beer.
    He goes to the fridge. Brings out two beers.
    I've been telling them for years that we should let the big
    ones go, put them into the Channel. But they don't want to
    know. They're not interested in turtles here.
WILLIAM: I see. But how . . . how do you think we would go
    about it?
GEORGE: Easy. Put them into the filters for about a week.
    Nobody would know they'd gone.
WILLIAM: You'd . . . help me then?

GEORGE: Like a shot.

WILLIAM: But wouldn't they bring charges against you?

GEORGE: No, no. They wouldn't bring charges. I'm Head
Keeper. I've been here for twenty-seven years. Anyway,
don't forget the RSPCA. If I said keeping giant turtles here
for thirty years was cruel, I don't think the Zoological
Society would take it too far. Anyway, I'd do it. What
about you?

WILLIAM *stares at him.*

Do you want to do it?

Pause.

WILLIAM: Yes.

GEORGE: Well, let's do it. I'll let you know a couple of days in
advance when we're going to clean the tank.

EXT. AQUARIUM. DAY

GEORGE *and* WILLIAM *emerge into sunlight. They stand a moment.*

EXT. ZOO

NEAERA *approaching. She sees* WILLIAM *and* GEORGE *talking.
She stops.*

EXT. AQUARIUM

GEORGE: I'll give you a tip. Take them down to Cornwall.

WILLIAM: Why?

GEORGE: Well, it gives them a head start. They've got a long
way to go.

EXT. ZOO

WILLIAM *walks towards the exit. He sees* NEAERA.

NEAERA *walks towards* WILLIAM.

NEAERA'S FACE

WILLIAM'S FACE

INT. AQUARIUM

It seems to be empty. NEAERA *walks towards George's office door. It
is ajar. She looks in. He is writing at a table. He looks up.*

NEAERA: Good morning.
GEORGE: Morning.
NEAERA: I wondered . . .
GEORGE: Yes?
NEAERA: That man . . . who was here just now . . . I saw him going out . . .
GEORGE: That's right. Tall chap.
NEAERA: I keep seeing him here.
GEORGE: Yes, he comes here quite a lot.
NEAERA: May I ask why?
GEORGE: He's interested in the turtles.
NEAERA: In what way?
GEORGE: He doesn't think they should be here.
NEAERA: Where does he think they should be?
GEORGE: In the sea.

INT. AQUARIUM
NEAERA *standing alone. She suddenly discerns two figures by a tank, a man and a* GIRL. *The man is murmuring. The* GIRL *whispers.*
GIRL: No. It's too late. It's too late.

NEAERA'S FACE, STRICKEN

WILLIAM SITTING IN HIS ROOM, STILL. NIGHT

NEAERA'S FACE

INT. BOOKSHOP. DAY
NEAERA *comes in. She sees* WILLIAM. *He nods. She goes to the Natural History shelves. Opens books without seeing them. He approaches, stands with her, sorts books. She looks at him.*
NEAERA: I wonder if you've time . . . for a word?
WILLIAM: Of course. What about a drink? In about five minutes?
NEAERA: Oh, yes. Thank you.

INT. PUB. DAY
NEAERA *at table. A plate of sandwiches on the table.* WILLIAM *bringing drinks from the bar. He sits.*

WILLIAM: My name's Snow, by the way. William Snow.

NEAERA: Mine's Duncan, Neaera Duncan.

WILLIAM: Neaera Duncan?

NEAERA: Yes.

WILLIAM: *Gillian Vole, Delia Swallow* – all the little animals?

NEAERA: Yes.

WILLIAM: Well, well. How funny. I used to read your books to my girls.

NEAERA: Really?

WILLIAM: When they were little.

She laughs shortly.

NEAERA: Well . . . yes.

They drink.

WILLIAM: We've got them in the shop. Still popular. Got a new one coming out?

NEAERA: No.

Silence.

These turtles . . .

WILLIAM: Turtles?

NEAERA: You've been speaking to the Head Keeper.

He drinks.

I have too. A little.

Pause.

If you have any . . . plan . . . I'd like to come in with you.

WILLIAM: Plan? What kind of plan?

NEAERA: For releasing them.

WILLIAM: I don't follow you.

NEAERA: Putting them into the sea.

He laughs.

WILLIAM: What makes you think I have a plan to do that?

Pause.

A dream, perhaps. But that's not a plan.

NEAERA: Well . . . a dream.

They stare at each other.

What would you need – to make it real?

WILLIAM: You'd need the co-operation of the Head Keeper. You'd need crates – for the turtles. You'd need a van, and you'd need a very cool head. I haven't got any of those things. Well, that's not entirely true. I might have the co-operation of the Head Keeper.

She looks up.

You've done this kind of thing before, have you?

NEAERA: No. I haven't.

WILLIAM: You haven't touched your sandwich. (*He drinks.*)
You like turtles, do you?

NEAERA: They're in prison.

WILLIAM: They're not alone in that.

Pause.

You could always write to *The Times* about it.

NEAERA: Nobody's interested in turtles. Except the Head
Keeper. And me. (*She looks at him.*) And you.

He drinks, smiles.

INT. WILLIAM'S HOUSE. BATHROOM

A piece of paper taped to a wall: 'PLEASE CLEAN BATH AFTER
USE'.

MISS NEAP *reading this. She leaves the bathroom.*

She crosses the landing, knocks on William's door. He opens it.

WILLIAM: Yes?

MISS NEAP: Did you put up that notice?

WILLIAM: Notice?

MISS NEAP: In the bathroom.

WILLIAM: Oh. Yes. Yes, I did.

MISS NEAP: I always clean the bath.

WILLIAM: Oh . . . I know . . .

MISS NEAP: Always.

WILLIAM: It wasn't meant for you, it was meant for him.

MISS NEAP: I've never been so upset.

WILLIAM: It wasn't meant for you. It was meant for *him*.

MISS NEAP: Who?

WILLIAM: *Him!*

MISS NEAP: Well, why didn't you say so, on the wall?

WILLIAM: Yes . . . sorry . . . I should have done that.

She walks away.

EXT. THE COMMON. NIGHT

WILLIAM *sitting. Orange sky. London hum.*

INT. WILLIAM'S HOUSE. HALL. DAY
WILLIAM *flipping through Yellow Pages. He finds Van Hire.*
Dozens of entries. Looks over them.
Suddenly a sound from above. He turns, looks up the stairs.

SANDOR LOOKING DOWN AT HIM
SANDOR *turns away. Footsteps on landing, door slams.*

WILLIAM SHUTS THE DIRECTORY

EXT. STREET. EVENING
Woman with greyhound, followed by man dragging leg.

EXT. HOUSE. EVENING
WILLIAM *at his window, looking down.*

EXT. STATIONARY TUBE TRAIN. DAY
The train stands in a station above ground. A pigeon on the
platform.

INT. TUBE TRAIN
The carriage almost empty. WILLIAM *sitting. The train hums. The*
pigeon walks in. Doors close. The train moves.
A MAN: Bloody pigeon. Christ!
    WILLIAM *watches the pigeon.*
    The train stops. Dark station. Doors open. Pigeon walks out.
    Doors close. Train moves.
    WILLIAM's *face against blurred, moving background.*

NEAERA SWIMMING IN THE OCEAN
A white shadow coming up from below. A shark, growing closer.
NEAERA: (*Voice over*) This isn't mine, this isn't mine!

INT. NEAERA'S FLAT. NIGHT
She is asleep in a chair. She sits up, abruptly, murmurs.
NEAERA: Not mine.
    She looks at a clock. The time: 3.45. Silence.

BEETLE IN TANK

Plants shrouded in green webs of algae. White, ghostly strands of old meat. Plastic shipwreck.

INT. NEAERA'S FLAT. NIGHT
NEAERA *opens the telephone directory. She flips to the letter S. She finds a list of seven W. Snows. She looks at the telephone, does not move.*

EXT. THE SQUARE. NIGHT
NEAERA *is sitting on a bench. A* POLICEMAN *approaches her.*
POLICEMAN: Morning.
NEAERA: Is it?
POLICEMAN: Well, it will be soon. Getting some air?
NEAERA: Yes. It's very close.
POLICEMAN: Feeling all right?
NEAERA: Yes. Thank you.
POLICEMAN: Do you live near here?
NEAERA: (*Gesturing*) In that house.
POLICEMAN: Ah. Well, good morning.

NEAERA'S POINT OF VIEW
The POLICEMAN *walking away. His steps echo.*

INT. NEAERA'S FLAT. DAWN
NEAERA *opening the windows. She looks at the telephone directory, still open at the list of Snows. She looks at her clock: 5.00. She sits down, lights a cigarette.*

EXT. MUSEUM STREET. DAY
A bus stops at bus stop. NEAERA *gets off. She walks towards the bookshop.*
The bookshop is closed, dark. She walks up and down the street, looking in other shops.
HARRIET *drives up in a Citroën Deux-Chevaux. She goes to the shop, unlocks the door, goes in, locks the door.* NEAERA *goes to the window, looks in.* HARRIET *turns the lights on. She picks up the post, notices* NEAERA, *takes post to the inner office.*
NEAERA *stands.*
HARRIET *returns with brown-paper bags, puts money into the till.*

She sees NEAERA *again, looks at her watch, goes to the door, unlocks it.*
NEAERA: Good morning.
HARRIET: Good morning.
    NEAERA *goes in.*

INT. BOOKSHOP. DAY
HARRIET: Can I help you?
NEAERA: Will Mr Snow be in today?
HARRIET: It's his day off.
NEAERA: Could you give me his phone number? It's urgent.
HARRIET: I'm sorry. I'm afraid I can't do that.
NEAERA: I think he may be ill.
HARRIET: Ill?
NEAERA: Would you ring him yourself – just to make sure he's
    all right?
HARRIET: He looked perfectly all right yesterday.
NEAERA: It's urgent.
HARRIET: But if you're a friend of his, you'd have his number.
    NEAERA *stares at her blankly.*
    All right, I'll ring him. Who shall I say it is?
NEAERA: Neaera Duncan.
HARRIET: What, the one who does the *Gillian Vole* books?
NEAERA: Yes.
HARRIET: (*Smiling*) We stock them here, you know. Hold on a
    minute.
    HARRIET *goes into the office.* NEAERA *watches her dialling
    through the window.*
    HARRIET *puts the receiver down, scribbling on a piece of
    paper. She comes out.*
    No answer.
NEAERA: No answer?
HARRIET: Do you want his address?
    She gives NEAERA *the piece of paper.*
NEAERA: Oh. Thank you.
HARRIET: He's probably asleep.
NEAERA: It isn't personal . . . you know. I mean . . . it's
    nothing personal at all, really.
HARRIET: Well, there's his address anyway.

NEAERA: Thank you.
She leaves the shop.

EXT. MUSEUM STREET
A taxi. NEAERA *hails it, gets into it.*

INT. TAXI. MOVING
DRIVER: Do you know the street?
NEAERA: No. Don't you?
DRIVER: I'm a suburban driver. I don't know London. I'm a
    Jehovah's Witness. We think God's going to step in and
    put things right in a couple of years. There won't be any
    taxis then.
NEAERA: What will there be?
DRIVER: The Lord will take care of the righteous. We've been
    interested in the year 1986 for some time.
NEAERA: What will you do if nothing happens in 1986?
DRIVER: A lot of people ask that question. I'll tell you –
    *They pass very loud road works. The road works drown his
    voice.*
NEAERA: What?
DRIVER: The Lord will provide.
NEAERA: I think it's somewhere off Fulham Broadway.
    He turns and looks at her.

EXT. WILLIAM'S HOUSE. DAY
The taxi draws up. NEAERA *gets out. She goes up the steps, rings
the bell.*
MRS INCHCLIFF *opens the door.*
MRS INCHCLIFF: Yes?
NEAERA: Is Mr Snow here?
MRS INCHCLIFF: Yes. Right up to the top.
    NEAERA *goes in.*

INT. WILLIAM'S HOUSE
NEAERA *goes up the stairs. At the top landing she stands, lost.*
SANDOR *is at the cooker, stirring a saucepan. He stares at her.*
NEAERA: Mr Snow?
    He points to a door.

SANDOR: That one.
　　She knocks on the door. WILLIAM *opens it.*
WILLIAM: Good Lord! Hello. What a surprise.
　　She stares at him.
　　Come in.

INT. WILLIAM'S ROOM
He closes the door.
WILLIAM: What's the trouble? You look done in. Have some
　　coffee. Sit down.
　　He pours coffee. Gives it to her. She sips.
　　What is it? You don't look well.
NEAERA: I'm sorry, I've never done anything like this before,
　　you must think I'm mad, they gave me your address at the
　　shop, I said it was urgent, she was very nice –
WILLIAM: Urgent? What?
NEAERA: Don't be angry. I know I don't know you, we don't
　　know each other – but I –
WILLIAM: Drink your coffee.
NEAERA: It was a dream. Nonsense, of course, anyway I
　　couldn't sleep, I mean I wasn't in bed, just dropped off, in
　　a chair, I couldn't sleep, you see, I must have dropped off,
　　it was the middle of the night, there was this shark coming
　　up out of the depths, in the sea, green water, a white
　　glimmer, a shark, it woke me up, coming towards me, I
　　woke up –
WILLIAM: A shark?
NEAERA: Yes.
　　He gives her a cigarette and lights it.
WILLIAM: Drink your coffee.
　　She inhales the cigarette.
NEAERA: I have my own cigarettes, in my bag.
WILLIAM: You had this dream . . . of a shark?
NEAERA: Yes.
WILLIAM: And what does that mean?
NEAERA: Death.
　　Pause.
WILLIAM: Does it?
NEAERA: Yes.

WILLIAM: Well . . . how awful. How awful for you.

NEAERA: No. It wasn't mine.

WILLIAM: What?

NEAERA: It wasn't mine.

WILLIAM: What do you mean?

NEAERA: It was yours.

WILLIAM: My what?

NEAERA: Your death.

Pause.

WILLIAM: Oh, thanks. (*Pause.*) How do you know?

NEAERA: I knew.

WILLIAM: But this shark . . . was coming up through the water towards *you*. You said that. So where do I come into it?

NEAERA: No. It was coming up through the water towards you.

He laughs.

WILLIAM: Jesus Christ.

Silence.

So you came here because you thought I was dead? You thought I'd done myself in? Well, here I am, as you see. In the pink. (*He sits.*) As you see.

She smokes.

NEAERA: You see, they do say that when you dream of yourself you're actually dreaming about someone else.

WILLIAM: Yes. Nice and convenient, that. As a theory. I must remember that.

NEAERA: Anyway, I think we should forget all about these turtles.

WILLIAM: You've taken the words out of my mouth.

NEAERA: It's ridiculous.

WILLIAM: Dangerous too. You know that big male? He could take your hand off with one bite. Probably will, too. Irritation. I mean, they haven't actually *said* they want to swim back to Ascension Island, have they? Probably quite comfortable where they are. After all, they've been there for thirty years. You get used to things.

NEAERA: Yes. That's right.

INT. BOOKSHOP. MORNING

HARRIET *in the office, making tea.* WILLIAM *reading a paper.*

HARRIET: Did Miss Duncan ever reach you?

WILLIAM: Oh, yes. She did.

HARRIET: Was it all right, giving her your address?

WILLIAM: Yes, fine. Silly of me not to have given it to her before.

HARRIET: I didn't know she was a friend of yours.

WILLIAM: Haven't known her long.

HARRIET: Funny, meeting authors.

She pours water into the pot.

WILLIAM: That's a pretty dress.

HARRIET: Oh. Thank you.

INT. PUB. EVENING

WILLIAM *and* HARRIET *at a table (the same table as* WILLIAM *and* NEAERA).

HARRIET: I thought you'd never ask.

WILLIAM: Ask what?

HARRIET: Me. Out.

WILLIAM: Oh. Yes. Did I?

HARRIET: Yes. You did.

WILLIAM: I thought you asked me.

HARRIET: Well, perhaps I did.

They drink.

Do you like working in the bookshop?

WILLIAM: I love it. Love it. I love all the shapes and sizes.

HARRIET: What, of the books?

WILLIAM: No. The customers.

HARRIET: Oh, do you?

WILLIAM: Don't you?

HARRIET: If you don't like it, why do you stay?

WILLIAM: Ah. Well, I did have ambitions once. I was going to discover the Amazon.

HARRIET: Hasn't it been discovered?

WILLIAM: Yes. (*Pause.*) You're nice anyway.

INT. RESTAURANT. EVENING

WILLIAM *and* HARRIET *at table, sitting with food and two bottles of wine, one empty, one half empty.*

HARRIET: Have you ever been married?

WILLIAM: I must have been. I had two daughters. They were
little once. They used to sit on my lap.

HARRIET: Were you a good father?

WILLIAM: They thought so. But they were only children at the
time. Yes, I was married. I was 'in business'. Out in the
big world. A long time ago. Didn't like any of it. So I
thought I'd find a nice little corner, in a nice little
bookshop, and keep out of trouble. See?

HARRIET: No.

WILLIAM: What about you? Are you going to go far?

HARRIET: Why not? Don't you think I'm intelligent?

WILLIAM: Very.

HARRIET: And capable?

WILLIAM: Very. I think you'll go far.

    He pours wine.

HARRIET: What about women?

WILLIAM: What about them?

HARRIET: What *about* them?

WILLIAM: Oh, *women.* No, no.

HARRIET: What do you mean, no, no?

WILLIAM: I've been on a sabbatical for years.

HARRIET: Why?

    He drinks.

    Don't you miss it sometimes?

WILLIAM: It? Oh . . . *it.* Yes, I suppose I do miss it,
sometimes.

HARRIET: Might as well get some fun out of life.

WILLIAM: Is that your motto?

HARRIET: It obviously isn't yours.

WILLIAM: Oh, I don't know. Here we are. Painting the town
red.

HARRIET: I saw *Les Enfants du Paradis* the other day. Do you
remember what Arletty says?

WILLIAM: What?

HARRIET: C'est si simple, l'amour.

WILLIAM: Funny lot, the French.

EXT. WILLIAM'S HOUSE. NIGHT
Harriet's car draws up.

INT. CAR. NIGHT
HARRIET: Don't you want to come to my place?
WILLIAM: No. You'll love my place.

INT. WILLIAM'S HOUSE
WILLIAM *and* HARRIET *creeping up the stairs. They peer round the top landing.* SANDOR *making coffee. He stares.*
HARRIET: (*Cheerfully*) Hello.
    They go into the room.

INT. WILLIAM'S ROOM. NIGHT
The door closes. Lamplight through the window. He kisses her. She whispers.
HARRIET: Remember Arletty.

INT. WILLIAM'S ROOM. MORNING
Church bells.
HARRIET *and* WILLIAM *naked in bed. She is asleep. He looks down at her. A knock on the door.* MRS INCHCLIFF'*s voice.*
MRS INCHCLIFF: (*Voice over*) Telephone.
    HARRIET *wakes up.*
WILLIAM: Telephone.
    He gets up, puts on a dressing-gown, goes out.

INT. HALL
WILLIAM *comes downstairs, picks up the telephone.* MRS INCHCLIFF *glimpsed in her workroom in background.*
WILLIAM: Hello?
GEORGE: (*Voice over*) This is George Fairbairn.
WILLIAM: Oh, hello.
GEORGE: (*Voice over*) The big day is coming up, Thursday week.
WILLIAM: Ah. I see.
GEORGE: (*Voice over*) Are you still on?
WILLIAM: Yes. Yes.
GEORGE: (*Voice over*) You'll need crates. Do you want the measurements?
WILLIAM: Oh. Right. Right. Just a minute.
    He picks up pad and pencil.

Yes. Right.

GEORGE: (*Voice over*) Four feet long, twenty-eight inches wide, one foot deep.

WILLIAM: Right.

GEORGE: (*Voice over*) If you can drop the crates off, I'll have them boxed and ready for pick-up.

WILLIAM: OK. Right.

GEORGE: (*Voice over*) Drop them off about seven, Thursday week.

WILLIAM: Right.

GEORGE: (*Voice over*) See you then.

WILLIAM: Oh, listen. I'll ring to confirm.

GEORGE: (*Voice over*) Confirm?

MISS NEAP *comes down the stairs and goes to the hall table.*

WILLIAM: Yes.

GEORGE: (*Voice over*) I thought you had confirmed.

WILLIAM: Just . . . give me a few days.

GEORGE: (*Voice over*) Do you want to scrub round it?

WILLIAM: Just give me a couple of days.

GEORGE: (*Voice over*) All right. Ring me in a couple of days then.

Phone down.

WILLIAM: Morning, Miss Neap.

MISS NEAP: Good morning.

She picks up the Sunday Express *from the hall table. He goes up the stairs.*

INT. WILLIAM'S ROOM

WILLIAM *enters. Gets into bed.*

HARRIET: Who was it?

WILLIAM: No one.

She touches his face.

INT. HALL

MISS NEAP *with the* Sunday Express *in her hand, looking at herself in the hall mirror.*

INT. BOOKSHOP. DAY

A large American WOMAN *and a small American man enter the shop. The* WOMAN *approaches* MR MEAGER. *In background, in a corner of the shop,* WILLIAM *and* HARRIET *are whispering.*

WOMAN: I want to look at some guide books. You have guide books?

MR MEAGER: Certainly. Which part of England?

WOMAN: William Shakespeare country.

MR MEAGER: Miss Sims, would you help this lady? Guide book to the Cotswolds.

HARRIET: Oh, yes.

WOMAN: (*To* HUSBAND) You go and buy some antiques or something. Come back in ten minutes.

HUSBAND: Sure thing.

He goes towards the door.

NEAERA *comes in.*

Pardon me.

He lets her pass.

HARRIET: (*To* WOMAN) Over here.

She leads WOMAN *to a table.*

WILLIAM *sees* NEAERA. *She goes to the Poetry section.*

HARRIET *glances at her.*

WOMAN: (*To* HARRIET) You know a place called Hog's Bottom?

HARRIET: No, I . . .

WOMAN: Isn't it close by Stratford-upon-Avon?

HARRIET: It could be, easily.

WILLIAM *has moved across to* NEAERA. *She looks at him. They speak quietly.*

NEAERA: Have you thought any more – about the matter?

WILLIAM: I thought we agreed –

NEAERA: We didn't agree anything.

WOMAN: (*To* HARRIET) OK, give me two of those and one of those. Where the hell's my husband?

NEAERA: Have you spoken to the man?

WILLIAM: Well . . . yes. He phoned.

NEAERA: With what news?

WILLIAM: Thursday week . . . is the day.

HARRIET *gives the* WOMAN *her books, takes cash.*

HARRIET: Thank you, madam.

HUSBAND *enters shop.*

WOMAN: Where have you been?

She gives him package.
Take this.
They go out.
NEAERA *goes towards the door.*
HARRIET: Hello.
NEAERA: Oh, hello.
She goes out.
WILLIAM *stands by* HARRIET.
WILLIAM: I've got to have a drink with her.
HARRIET: Why?
WILLIAM *does not reply, sorts a pile of books.*

INT. PUB. DAY
WILLIAM *and* NEAERA *at the table.*
Silence.
WILLIAM: So you . . . you want to do it.
NEAERA: Yes.
Pause.
WILLIAM: How do you know I'm competent?
NEAERA: I don't.
WILLIAM: And what about you?
NEAERA: I don't know.
Pause.
WILLIAM: I think it's crazy. We could end up in prison. Or
worse.
NEAERA: Well, don't do it.
WILLIAM: No. All right. We'll do it.
They sit.

INT. HARRIET'S CAR, MOVING. NIGHT
HARRIET: Oh, I got those tickets.
WILLIAM: What tickets?
HARRIET: For the Queen Elizabeth Hall.
WILLIAM: Oh, yes. Yes.
HARRIET: There are eight altogether.
WILLIAM: Eight what?
HARRIET: Recitals! Have you forgotten?
WILLIAM: No, no. Great.

She drives.
Eight, eh?

INT. RESTAURANT. BOOTHS. NIGHT
NEAERA *in a booth, alone. The booth shakes as people sit in the next booth.*
NEAERA *has finished her meal. She sits with wine, coffee and a book.*
WILLIAM's *and* HARRIET's *voices from the next booth.*
WILLIAM: (*Voice over*) What are you going to have?
HARRIET: (*Voice over*) I don't know.
WILLIAM: (*Voice over*) I'm having Steak au poivre.
HARRIET: (*Voice over*) Where's that? I can't see it.
WILLIAM: (*Voice over*) There. Down there.
HARRIET: (*Voice over*) Oh yes. Oh I . . . no, I'll have scampi.
WILLIAM: (*Voice over*) Scampi. Provençal?
    NEAERA *finishes her wine and stands.*
HARRIET: (*Voice over*) No . . . yes. Provençal. That's rice, isn't it?
WILLIAM: (*Voice over*) More or less.
HARRIET: (*Voice over*) (*Laughs.*) More or less?
    NEAERA *moves past the booth, looks at the couple with a prepared smile. They look up. They are not William and Harriet.*

INT. HARRIET's FLAT. NIGHT
HARRIET *lying in* WILLIAM's *arms. They are naked. She kisses him.*
HARRIET: We've been invited to a party.
WILLIAM: We?
HARRIET: Yes.
WILLIAM: Who by?
HARRIET: Nick and Ros. They want to meet you.
WILLIAM: When?
HARRIET: Saturday.
WILLIAM: No. I can't. I'm sorry. I've got some odd jobs to do. I've told myself I'm going to do them on Saturday, you see. I've set Saturday aside.

HARRIET: Odd jobs?
WILLIAM: Yes.
    Pause.
HARRIET: What does that woman want?
WILLIAM: What woman?
HARRIET: Miss Duncan.
WILLIAM: Nothing. She doesn't want anything.
HARRIET: Nothing?
WILLIAM: Nothing.

INT. TELEPHONE BOX. EARLY EVENING
WILLIAM *talking.*
WILLIAM: Wait a minute. Just a second. I'm making a note:
    £15.99p a day, 7p a mile, £80 deposit?
VOICE: That's right.
WILLIAM: Right. That's OK.
VOICE: Right.
WILLIAM: Thursday the fourteenth.
VOICE: Thursday the fourteenth. Got it.
WILLIAM: Thank you.
VOICE: Right. OK, Mr Quinn.
    WILLIAM *puts the telephone down, picks it up, dials another*
    number.
    He suddenly sees MISS NEAP *walking along the pavement. He*
    turns away. He puts a coin in. GEORGE's *voice.*
GEORGE: (*Voice over*) Hello.
WILLIAM: Mr Fairbairn?
GEORGE: (*Voice over*) Yes.
WILLIAM: It's William Snow.
GEORGE: (*Voice over*) Oh, hello.
    WILLIAM *looks over his shoulder, sees* MISS NEAP *stroking a*
    cat on the pavement. He turns back to the telephone.
WILLIAM: Thursday's fine.
GEORGE: (*Voice over*) Oh is it? Good.
WILLIAM: I'll be there.
GEORGE: (*Voice over*) Good.
WILLIAM: That lady will be with me.
GEORGE: (*Voice over*) Lady?

WILLIAM: Yes. You know her.

GEORGE: (*Voice over*) Oh, her? Yes. Right. Good. Safety in numbers.

WILLIAM: I hope you're right.

GEORGE: (*Voice over*) It'll go like clockwork. How about the crates?

WILLIAM: They'll be there.

GEORGE: (*Voice over*) I hope so. Otherwise they'll be sitting on your lap.

WILLIAM: Bye.

GEORGE: (*Voice over*) Bye.

INT. BOOKSHOP. EVENING

The shop is closed. MR MEAGER *and* WILLIAM. HARRIET *in background.*

MR MEAGER: Yes, he's made a remarkable recovery, as a matter of fact.

WILLIAM: Oh good.

MR MEAGER: I was quite taken aback, when they told me he was still alive. I thought he was a doomed man myself. Oh well, good night.

WILLIAM *and* HARRIET: Good night.

    MR MEAGER *goes out.*

    WILLIAM *and* HARRIET *turn out the lights in silence.*

WILLIAM: Right, then.

HARRIET: Well, have a good time . . . with your odd jobs.

    He goes to the door.

EXT. BOOKSHOP. EVENING

HARRIET *locks up. They stand.*

HARRIET: Want a lift?

WILLIAM: No. It's all right. I'll walk up to the station. (*Pause.*) Are you going to the party?

HARRIET: I don't know.

    Pause.

WILLIAM: Well . . . till Monday.

HARRIET: Yes.

    He kisses her lightly, turns away. She gets into her car.

INT. CAR
HARRIET *driving. The car passes* WILLIAM, *walking. She does not turn.*

INT. TUBE TRAIN. DAY
WILLIAM *sitting with planks of wood. The train stops. The doors open.* WILLIAM, *with some difficulty, carries the planks through the door.*

INT. WILLIAM'S HOUSE. HALL. DAY
Planks of wood leaning against the wall. WILLIAM, *carrying planks, opens the front door, leans planks against the wall.*

INT. WILLIAM'S HOUSE. WORKROOM. EVENING
WILLIAM *sawing wood with a hand saw. He is surrounded by wood. On a chest lie rope and ring bolts.*
MRS INCHCLIFF *comes in.*
MRS INCHCLIFF: What are you making?
WILLIAM: Turtle crates. I'm going to steal three sea turtles from the Zoo and put them into the sea.
MRS INCHCLIFF: Sounds a good thing to do. Nice to have a man doing something in here again. Charlie was never out of here. Do you want to try his Black and Decker?
She goes to a cupboard and brings it out.
Here.
WILLIAM *looks at it.*
WILLIAM: Frighten the life out of me, these things.
MRS INCHCLIFF: Try it.
He does.
MRS INCHCLIFF: What do you think?
WILLIAM: It works.

INT. MISS NEAP'S ROOM. NIGHT
MISS NEAP *sitting alone. Hammering from below.*

MRS INCHCLIFF'S KITCHEN. NIGHT
MRS INCHCLIFF *is making tea and sandwiches. Hammering above. She puts the plates on a tray. The hammering stops. She looks up.*

INT. WORKROOM. NIGHT
The three crates are finished. Open boxes, no lids. MRS INCHCLIFF
comes in with tray. She surveys crates.
WILLIAM: What do you think?
MRS INCHCLIFF: Beautiful.
WILLIAM: With tools you can do anything.
MRS INCHCLIFF: With tools and a man.
    MISS NEAP *comes downstairs. She looks round the door, sees*
    crates.
MISS NEAP: What lovely things. What are you going to put into
    them?
WILLIAM: Turtles. I'm going to put some sea turtles into them
    and take them down to the sea.
MISS NEAP: Ah, the sea. Yes. It always seems so far away. Even
    though the Thames goes into it.
    The front door closes. SANDOR *appears, looks round the door.*
    He carries newspapers under his arm and a packed briefcase.
SANDOR: Good evening.
    He sees the crates, goes to them, examines them, looks at
    WILLIAM.
SANDOR: You did this?
WILLIAM: That's right.
SANDOR: Quite good.
WILLIAM: Thanks.
SANDOR: Quite good.

INT. WILLIAM'S ROOM. EVENING
WILLIAM *looking out of the window.*
The lights of the tube train.
The woman with the greyhound walking slowly along the pavement.
No man.
He turns from the window.

INT. NEAERA'S HOUSE. DAY
NEAERA *ringing the bell of Johnson's flat. He opens the door. He is*
wearing a sweater.
JOHNSON: Oh, hello. How are you?
NEAERA: You're here. Oh good. I wasn't sure.
JOHNSON: Yes, I'm here this week.

NEAERA: Well, could you possibly feed my beetle? I have to be
away Thursday and Friday –
JOHNSON: Of course.
NEAERA: Thank you so much. There's a sort of lamb chop –
well, the remains –
JOHNSON: Yes. Quite.
NEAERA: Here's the key.
JOHNSON: First rate. It will be an honour.
*She gives him the key. A sudden male cough from inside
Johnson's flat. She looks at* JOHNSON. *He smiles.*
Would you like to show me where the remains . . . are?
NEAERA: Remains?
JOHNSON: Of the lamb chop.
NEAERA: Oh yes. Of course.
He follows her to her door. They go into her flat.

INT. NEAERA'S FLAT. SITTING-ROOM
On the table a large map spread out. NEAERA *goes into the kitchen.*
JOHNSON *follows.*
NEAERA: There.
JOHNSON: Ah. Right. It will be done.
NEAERA: Thank you.
They go back into the sitting-room.
JOHNSON: I do think you're a wonderful mother to your beetle.
She laughs.
JOHNSON *notices a large book on turtles open on the table. He
looks at it, then at the map.*
Going somewhere nice?
NEAERA: Cornwall.
JOHNSON: Cornwall? Really? I was born there.
NEAERA: Really?
JOHNSON: Yes, I was born in Cornwall.
He smiles.

INT. BOOKSHOP. DAY
WILLIAM *and* MR MEAGER. HARRIET *in background.*
WILLIAM: (*To* MR MEAGER) Listen, I wonder if you'd mind if I
took Friday off. Personal matter. Illness.
MR MEAGER: Serious?

WILLIAM: Well . . . you know . . .

MR MEAGER: Family?

WILLIAM: First cousin.

MR MEAGER: Heart?

WILLIAM: No. Feet.

MR MEAGER: Feet?

WILLIAM: Gout.

MR MEAGER: Ah. Can be nasty.

WILLIAM: I don't trust doctors.

MR MEAGER: Quite right. Yes, yes. That'll be all right.

He moves away.

HARRIET *joins* WILLIAM, *whispers.*

HARRIET: What is it?

WILLIAM: Nothing.

HARRIET: Where are you going?

WILLIAM: It's private.

HARRIET: Look, you're not compelled to tell me anything at all, you're quite entitled to take a day off without having to –

WILLIAM: Look –

HARRIET: – without having to explain yourself to me, you're a perfectly free man, I just asked, that's all, I realize I shouldn't have asked –

WILLIAM: Harriet –

HARRIET: I'm quite grown up you know –

WILLIAM: I know, but –

HARRIET: I still like you, whether you – whatever you –

WILLIAM: Everything isn't sex. There are other things that are private.

A customer enters the shop. HARRIET *goes towards him.*

HARRIET: (*Brightly*) Yes, sir. Can I help you?

EXT. ZOO. DAY

Camera moves across the Zoo. A telephone is ringing.

INT. ZOO: RECEPTION

The telephone is ringing. A MAN *picks it up.*

MAN: Zoo here.

WILLIAM: (*Voice over*) Hello, is that the Zoo?

MAN: Zoo here.

The following sequence is intercut between WILLIAM *in a coin box and the receptionist.* MAN *in Zoo's reception.*

WILLIAM: I think you should be warned. I'm going to steal some of your animals.

MAN: Oh yes? What kind of animals?

WILLIAM: Big ones.

MAN: When are you going to do it?

WILLIAM: Soon.

MAN: How are you going to do it?

WILLIAM: I'm not going to tell you.

MAN: I see. Well, thanks for letting us know.

WILLIAM: Not at all.

EXT. NEAERA'S HOUSE. EARLY EVENING

NEAERA *stands with two suitcases.*

WILLIAM *draws up in a large van. He gets out.*

WILLIAM: Hello. We'll put your cases in the back. What have you got in there?

NEAERA: Blankets, pillows.

WILLIAM: Oh.

He opens the back of the van. Three crates. Rope, etc. Blankets and pillows.

INT. VAN

NEAERA *sitting in passenger seat.* WILLIAM *climbs in.*

NEAERA: The crates are beautiful.

WILLIAM: Oh good. Listen, I'm very nervous about this van. I've never sat so high up for a start. But the most important thing is – I – you see – it's the width. It's so wide. I'm not used to it. Will you tell me if I'm too close to parked cars, or the kerb – as we go?

NEAERA: Yes.

WILLIAM: Thank you.

EXT. LONDON STREET

Van being driven slowly down the street. Rain.

INT. VAN

WILLIAM: Where the hell are the bloody wipers?

He tries various switches, finds wipers.

NEAERA: Too close!

WILLIAM: Blast!

He veers away.

EXT. ZOO. WORKS GATE. EVENING

GEORGE *standing with a trolley. Van draws up.* WILLIAM *gets out, goes to the back door.* GEORGE *goes to Neaera's window. She winds the window down.*

GEORGE: Good evening.

NEAERA: (*Smiling*) Good evening.

GEORGE *to back door. They take out the crates and put them on the trolley.*

WILLIAM: Are they all right?

GEORGE: Perfection.

WILLIAM: See you at eight.

GEORGE: I'll be here. So will they.

INT. KEBAB HOUSE. EVENING

WILLIAM *and* NEAERA *at a table. Greek music, a candle, retsina.*

WILLIAM: Cheers.

NEAERA: Cheers.

WILLIAM: Here's to our friends.

NEAERA: Yes.

They drink.

Why did you choose Polperro?

WILLIAM: Oh, I don't know. Pretty name. Plenty of sea.

NEAERA: Yes.

WILLIAM: Do you agree?

NEAERA: Sounds fine.

WILLIAM: Do you keep animals?

NEAERA: I have a water beetle.

WILLIAM: Does she want to go to Polperro? She could ride on the back of the turtles.

NEAERA: She's a freshwater beetle. You know what her motto is?

WILLIAM: What?

NEAERA: East, West, Home's Best.

WILLIAM: But it's not our motto, is it?

NEAERA: No.
WILLIAM: Perhaps we can ride on the back of the turtles.
NEAERA: Bum a ride on the turtles?
WILLIAM: Is that what we're doing?
NEAERA: I don't know. I haven't really . . . thought.
WILLIAM: No. I haven't *thought*, either. Makes a change,
      doesn't it?
NEAERA: (*Grinning*) Yes, it does.

EXT. ZOO. WORKS GATE. EVENING
GEORGE *trundling a crate covered with tarpaulin on a trolley. He
places it beside another trolley covered with tarpaulin.
Another* KEEPER *passes.*
KEEPER: Hello, George. What you got in there?
GEORGE: Turtles.
KEEPER: Oh yes? What are you doing with them?
GEORGE: Giving them a holiday. They need it.
KEEPER: Well, I don't know if they bloody need it, but I bloody
      need it. See you.
      He goes.

INT. RESTAURANT
WAITER *with food.*
WAITER: Two Doner Kebabs.
      He sets them down, goes.
NEAERA: Looks delicious.
WILLIAM: We're going to need it. We have a long way to go.
NEAERA: How long?
WILLIAM: Two hundred and fifty miles.
NEAERA: I've packed a flask of coffee.
WILLIAM: Have you? So have I.
      She laughs.
NEAERA: Have you?

EXT. ZOO. WORKS GATE. EVENING
GEORGE *waiting with three trolleys covered with tarpaulin. The van
draws up.* WILLIAM *gets out, opens the back door. They take the
tarpaulins off, put the crates in the back of the van, followed by one
trolley.*

NEAERA *joins them. They all look at the turtles. They lie on their backs, with their flippers pressed against their sides, their mouths open. They sigh.*

NEAERA: So there they are.

WILLIAM: There they are.

GEORGE: Got the champagne?

WILLIAM: Champagne?

GEORGE: For the launching.

WILLIAM: I'll get some on the way.

GEORGE: I took the liberty of laying on a bottle. Give you both a little send-off.

INT. HEAD KEEPER'S OFFICE

GEORGE *opening champagne.*

GEORGE: It's not every day I send my turtles out into the world, you know. Something of an occasion.

He pours into stemmed glasses.

Here's to the launching.

NEAERA: Here's to you.

WILLIAM: Here's to us.

They all drink.

EXT. ZOO. WORKS GATE. NIGHT

WILLIAM *and* NEAERA *in the van.* GEORGE *saluting. The van moves.* GEORGE *suddenly shouts after them. The van stops abruptly.*

GEORGE *runs to the van.* WILLIAM *lowers his window.*

GEORGE: Don't forget to give them a bucket of water every three hours. To wet them down.

WILLIAM: Bucket? I haven't got a bucket.

GEORGE: Any garage. Easy.

WILLIAM: Every what?

NEAERA: Three hours.

GEORGE: Good luck.

WILLIAM *turns ignition. The van moves away.* NEAERA *waves.*

WILLIAM: (*Muttering*) A bucket every three hours!

EXT. BAKER STREET. NIGHT

Van moving. Rain.

EXT. BAYSWATER ROAD. NIGHT
Van moving.

EXT. OFF-LICENCE. HAMMERSMITH. NIGHT
The van is parked outside a brightly lit off-licence. WILLIAM *can be seen at the counter.*

INT. VAN
NEAERA *sitting.*
Sound of a police siren. A police car draws up, parks in front of the van. A policeman gets out, goes into the off-licence.

OFF-LICENCE
NEAERA's *point of view.*
Through the off-licence window, WILLIAM *at the counter, a woman wrapping a bottle of champagne. The policeman stands next to* WILLIAM. WILLIAM *looks at him, looks away. He gives the woman money. Man behind the counter gives the policeman cigarettes. Woman gives* WILLIAM *the champagne. Policeman gives the man money, takes cigarettes. Policeman and* WILLIAM *approach the door together. Policeman lets* WILLIAM *go first.* WILLIAM *emerges, comes to the van. Policeman stands, unwrapping cigarettes.* WILLIAM *gets into the van.*
WILLIAM: Christ!
    He drives away.

EXT. CHISWICK HIGH ROAD. NIGHT
Van driving.

INT. VAN
NEAERA *looking at map by torchlight.*
NEAERA: We stay on the M4 until after Swindon. Then we go
    through Chippenham, Trowbridge, Frome, Shepton
    Mallet, Glastonbury, Taunton, Exeter, Plymouth, across
    the Tamar, go through Looe, and there's Polperro.
    She looks out suddenly.
    Too close!
WILLIAM: Christ!
    He veers away.

EXT. CHISWICK ROUNDABOUT
The van goes round the roundabout, missing the A4.

INT. VAN. NIGHT
NEAERA: No. That's the North Circular. You missed it.
WILLIAM: Damn!

EXT. ROUNDABOUT
The van goes round again.

EXT. M4
The van driving.

INT. VAN
WILLIAM: Where's this from? (*Passionately*) 'Ship and boat
    diverged; the cold damp night breeze blew between; a
    screaming gull flew overhead; the two hulls wildly rolled;
    we gave three hearty cheers and blindly plunged like fate
    into the lone Atlantic.'
NEAERA: *Moby Dick.*
WILLIAM: Right!
    The van drives on.
NEAERA: Blindly plunged like fate into the lone M4.
    Pause.
WILLIAM: Yes, that's it.

THE TURTLES SIGHING

EXT. M4
The van driving.

EXT. DARK TOWN
The van driving through a narrow street.

INT. VAN
NEAERA: Too close!
WILLIAM: It's so bloody wide! I'm not used to driving a thing
    like this. I'm not used to driving at all. I haven't had a car
    for years.

NEAERA: You had a car once, did you?
WILLIAM: Once.
  Pause.
NEAERA: I'm sorry I can't drive.
WILLIAM: That's all right.
  Pause.
NEAERA: I think you're driving very well.
  They drive on.

EXT. LAYBY. LATE AT NIGHT
The van parked. A large articulated lorry.

INT. VAN
WILLIAM *and* NEAERA *drinking coffee, eating sandwiches.*
WILLIAM: Lovely sandwiches.
NEAERA: Oh, good.
WILLIAM: It didn't occur to me that you'd make sandwiches. I
  thought we'd have to find some in some lousy café.
NEAERA: Ah, well . . .
WILLIAM: Is this home-made bread?
NEAERA: You mean did I bake it myself?
WILLIAM: Yes.
NEAERA: No. I didn't.
WILLIAM: Ah.
NEAERA: But it is good bread.
WILLIAM: Bloody good. Good cheese too.
NEAERA: Cheese gives you strength.
WILLIAM: Does it?
  *A sudden knock on the van door. They jump. A face at the
  window.* WILLIAM *winds the window down.*
MAN: Got a light, mate?
WILLIAM: Light? Yes. Just a moment.
  He gets out of the van and closes the door. He gives the MAN *a
  light.*
MAN: Thanks. Nice night.

THE LIGHTED VAN. MAN'S POINT OF VIEW
NEAERA *sitting. In background the crates clearly discernible.*
WILLIAM: It is.

MAN: Going far?

WILLIAM: Somerset.

MAN: Do it often?

WILLIAM: What?

MAN: This trip.

WILLIAM: No. No, not very often.

MAN: What have you got in the back there? Coffins?

> WILLIAM *laughs.*

WILLIAM: Coffins? No, no. Not coffins.

MAN: Well, they look like coffins.

WILLIAM: Do they?

MAN: You'd be surprised the kind of people you get on the road
    sometimes. Particularly at night.

WILLIAM: Really?

MAN: Oh yes. Well, ta-ta.

WILLIAM: Good night.

> *The* MAN *goes towards the lorry.* WILLIAM *gets back into the
> van.*

INT. VAN

WILLIAM: Let's go.

> *They drive away.*

MAN IN LORRY

He smokes, watching the van drive away.

INT. VAN. DRIVING

WILLIAM: What's the time?

NEAERA: One o'clock.

WILLIAM: We've got to find a garage. We've got to find a bucket.
    No point in throwing three dead turtles into the sea.

> *She looks back.*

NEAERA: They're breathing.

EXT. COUNTRY ROAD. NIGHT

Van approaches a dark garage.

INT. VAN

NEAERA: Closed.

EXT. COUNTRY ROAD. NIGHT
Van approaches a dark garage.

INT. VAN
WILLIAM: Oh my God.

EXT. COUNTRY ROAD. NIGHT
Van approaching a lit garage.

INT. VAN
WILLIAM: Open.

EXT. GARAGE. NIGHT
WILLIAM *putting cap on petrol tank. He goes towards the pay booth.*

INT. PAY BOOTH
MAN *behind the counter.* WILLIAM *pays.*
WILLIAM: Do you have a bucket, by any chance?
MAN: A bucket?
WILLIAM: Yes.
MAN: A bucket.
    He crosses the room. Picks up a bucket.
    What about this?
WILLIAM: Thank you. Can I fill it with water?
MAN: Just outside. Bring the bucket back though, won't you?
WILLIAM: Of course.
MAN: It's not mine, you see. It belongs to the guv'nor's wife.
WILLIAM: Does it?
MAN: Yes. She'd be lost without her bucket.

EXT. GARAGE
WILLIAM *filling bucket. He goes to the back of the van, empties the bucket. He fills the bucket again. Empties it again.*

MAN IN BOOTH. WATCHING
WILLIAM *brings the bucket back into the booth.*
WILLIAM: Thank you very much.
MAN: Like it?

147

WILLIAM: What?
MAN: The bucket.
WILLIAM: Yes. Lovely.
MAN: It is a lovely bucket, yes.
WILLIAM: Good night.
  He walks to the door.

INT. VAN. NIGHT
WILLIAM *looks back at the turtles.*
WILLIAM: Do you think they've any idea?
NEAERA: No. But when they find themselves in the ocean they'll
  just do what turtles do in the ocean. That's what I think.
WILLIAM: Swim.
NEAERA: Yes.
WILLIAM: You think so? You sure they won't drown – out of
  shock?
  She looks at him.
  Well, we'll soon find out.
NEAERA: How soon?
WILLIAM: About fifty miles.

THE MOON. BROKEN CLOUDS

THE ROAD. CATS' EYES ON THE ROAD

WILLIAM DRIVING. NEAERA ASLEEP

EXT. THE TAMAR BRIDGE
The van crosses it.

INT. VAN
WILLIAM: (*Softly*) Christ.
NEAERA: What?
WILLIAM: We've forgotten something.
NEAERA: What?
WILLIAM: The tide. It might be out.

EXT. POLPERRO
The van comes downhill into Polperro.

INT. VAN
WILLIAM: We're here. What's the time?
NEAERA: Two-thirty.

THE VAN STOPS

INT. VAN. NIGHT
They look at Polperro in the moonlight.
Silence.

EXT. POLPERRO
They get out of the van, quietly, and walk towards the harbour.

INNER HARBOUR
The tide is in. Boats bobbing. WILLIAM *and* NEAERA *come round the corner. They speak together.*
WILLIAM and NEAERA: It's in!
 The wind hits them in the face. They run up an incline to the outer harbour.
 In the outer harbour, waves crashing, spray flying, sea breaking halfway up steps, wind, moon in quick clouds.

THE VAN
They run to the van, open the doors, take out the trolley. She steadies the trolley. He tips the first crate on to it. He hauls the trolley towards the harbour. She follows with rope.

EXT. HARBOUR. BREAKWATER. NIGHT
They ease the crate off the trolley and lower it with the rope through the ring bolts.

THE TURTLE'S FACE

WILLIAM UPENDS THE CRATE AND TILTS IT

THE TURTLE HITS THE WATER AND DIVES

WILLIAM AND NEAERA HUG AND KISS EACH OTHER

SECOND TURTLE ON THE TROLLEY

TROLLEY WHEELED TOWARDS HARBOUR

CRATE UPENDED

TURTLE DIVES

THIRD TURTLE ON THE TROLLEY

CRATE UPENDED

TURTLE DIVES

CRATES THROWN INTO THE SEA

THE SEA
Turtles swimming. In background, WILLIAM *and* NEAERA *on the breakwater. They run down to the beach and into the surf.*

THE BEACH
WILLIAM: The champagne!
    He runs back to the van. She stands, looking out to sea.
    He runs up the incline towards her, with bottle and two cups.
    The cork pops. The champagne flows.
NEAERA: Here's wishing them luck!
WILLIAM: To the turtles!
    They drink, and, giggling, drink again.

THE WAVES SILVER UNDER THE MOON

THE BEACH
WILLIAM *waves.*
WILLIAM: Bye bye!
    They finish the bottle, he hurls it into the sea.
    They hug each other.

EXT. CAR PARK. NIGHT
The van drives in quietly. Shafts of headlights illumine other vans and caravans. Silence. The van stops. The lights go off.
An owl. Distant sound of the sea.

INT. BACK OF VAN
They arrange the blankets and pillows.
They lie down, on their backs.
Silence.
WILLIAM: Well, we did it.
NEAERA: Yes. (*Pause.*) You were wonderful.
WILLIAM: Oh . . . I don't know. (*Pause.*) You were pretty good
    yourself.
NEAERA: Thank you. (*Pause.*) Good night.
WILLIAM: Good night.

EXT. CAR PARK. AFTERNOON
The car park is packed. Dozens of people, children. Refreshments
and souvenir stands at the entrance. Bright sun.

INT. VAN
NEAERA *wakes up. She turns over, sees* WILLIAM *still asleep. She*
looks out of the window, surveys the car-park scene. She gets up,
quietly leaves the van.

EXT. CAR PARK
NEAERA *threading her way through people.*

INT. VAN
WILLIAM *wakes up. He turns, sees Neaera's pillow. He sits up,*
looks out of the window. He opens the doors and gets out.

EXT. CAR PARK
WILLIAM *stands, frowning in the sun. He sees* NEAERA, *who is*
leaning against the car-park wall. He goes to her.
WILLIAM: How are you feeling?
NEAERA: All right.

EXT. HARBOUR
WILLIAM *and* NEAERA *walk along the harbour. The tide is out.*
Boats sitting in the mud. Broken glass and rubbish.
Fishermen on the quayside. Boxes of fish. WILLIAM *looks into the*
boxes, casually.

151

WILLIAM: (*To a* FISHERMAN) What time was the high tide?
  Could you tell me?
FISHERMAN: Seven o'clock in the morning.
WILLIAM: Thank you.
  They walk away and up to the breakwater.
  In the mud, spars of broken crates stuck.
  WILLIAM *turns to her.*
  They got away.

EXT. POLPERRO
The van leaving Polperro.

EXT. THE TAMAR BRIDGE. DAY
The van crossing the Tamar Bridge.

EXT. VAN MOVING. NIGHT

INT. VAN. NIGHT
WILLIAM *and* NEAERA *silent.*

INT. ROADSIDE CAFÉ. NIGHT
WILLIAM *and* NEAERA *at table, with tea.*
A bottle of ketchup.
The café is empty.

INT. VAN. NIGHT
WILLIAM *bent over the wheel.*

EXT. WILLIAM'S POINT OF VIEW
Flashing light, shadows, red tail-lights.

INT. VAN
WILLIAM: My eyes are going.
NEAERA: Why don't you stop?
WILLIAM: Let's get there.

EXT. HAMMERSMITH FLY-OVER
Van moving.

EXT. NEAERA'S HOUSE. NIGHT
The van drives up.

INT. VAN
WILLIAM *switches off the engine. They sit.*
NEAERA: Are you all right?
WILLIAM: A bit tired. What's the time?
NEAERA: Midnight. (*Pause.*) Have you kept track of the
    expenses?
WILLIAM: I'll add it all up after I take the van back tomorrow.
    She did twenty miles to the gallon, you know.
NEAERA: Did she? Good. Well, good night.
WILLIAM: Good night.
    They look at each other, briefly. She gets out. He jumps out.
    Your blankets – your pillows.
NEAERA: Oh yes.

EXT. VAN
They open the back doors, put blankets and pillows into the case.
WILLIAM: Is that it?
NEAERA: Yes. Thanks.
WILLIAM: No. Thank you.
NEAERA: Good night.
    He watches her go up the steps and into the house.

INT. NEAERA'S FLAT
*She enters. Puts the light on in the hall. The sitting-room door is
closed. She goes to it, opens it.*

INT. SITTING-ROOM
*Glow from the tank. A man's legs. A figure stands. She puts the
light on.* JOHNSON.
JOHNSON: Sorry to startle you. I dropped in a cleaning squad. I
    was just checking their work rate.
NEAERA: Cleaning squad?
JOHNSON: My snails.
NEAERA: Ah.
    She looks in the tank.

RED SNAILS IN TANK

INT. NEAERA'S FLAT. ROOM. NIGHT
JOHNSON: Sorry to startle you. Your beetle's in damn good
    form, I must say. Very jolly.
NEAERA: Thank you . . . for looking after her.
JOHNSON: Well, I'll say good night.
    He goes to the door, turns.
    Good trip?
NEAERA: Yes.
JOHNSON: Good. Good.
    He goes.
    She looks after him.

INT. WILLIAM'S ROOM. MORNING
WILLIAM *gets out of bed. He puts on a dressing-gown and leaves
the room.*

INT. BATHROOM
Hair and scum in the bath.
WILLIAM *staring down. He grits his teeth.*

INT. LANDING
WILLIAM *goes to the cooker.*
The cooker is grimed with food. He stares at it.
He goes across the landing to Sandor's door, knocks.
SANDOR *opens the door. He wears a dressing-gown and slippers.*
SANDOR: Yes?
WILLIAM: Too much!
SANDOR: What?
WILLIAM: Too much!
SANDOR: What are you saying?
WILLIAM: You clean that cooker.
SANDOR: Who clean cooker? Who say?
WILLIAM: *You* clean cooker. And bath! I say.
    WILLIAM *pokes him in the chest.*
SANDOR: Mind. Go slow. I caution you. Piss off. All best.
WILLIAM: No. Not all best. All bleeding worst.
    He grabs the lapel of Sandor's dressing-gown.
    Clean the cooker!
    SANDOR *turns* WILLIAM *round, thrusting his arm behind his*

back. WILLIAM *flings his arm back and hits* SANDOR *in the face. They both fall to the floor.*
SANDOR *gets* WILLIAM *in a scissors grip. He tightens his legs round* WILLIAM'*s ribs. They lie on the landing.*

WILLIAM'S FACE
It is pressed against the carpet. Sound of SANDOR *breathing above him. Sound of a train approaching.* WILLIAM'*s nose sniffing the carpet.*

EXT. THE COMMON. DAY
The train moving. Signals green. Red signals flash.

INT. LANDING
Sudden upheaval.
SANDOR *rolling down the stairs.*
WILLIAM *crouched on the landing.*

SANDOR
He stares up at WILLIAM.

WILLIAM
He stares down at SANDOR.
MRS INCHCLIFF *runs up the stairs.*
MRS INCHCLIFF: What's happening? Why is everyone lying on the floor?
    Silence.
SANDOR: We have collision. Down we tumble.
    MRS INCHCLIFF *looks up at* WILLIAM. *He looks down.*

INT. AQUARIUM. DAY
Empty turtle tank.
NEAERA *looking at it. She goes to the office door, knocks, enters.*
GEORGE *is there.*

INT. OFFICE
GEORGE: Hello! Come in. Sit down. You're back. How did it go? What happened?

NEAERA: They went. They went into the sea . . . and they went off.

GEORGE: Wonderful.

NEAERA: Unless you've had any reports – I mean of turtles being picked up, off the Cornish coast.

GEORGE: No reports.

NEAERA: Well . . . we did it.

GEORGE: That's terrific.

NEAERA: Yes. We did it.

She suddenly cries.

He puts his arm around her.

GEORGE: They'll be very pleased, you know.

NEAERA: (*Crying*) Who?

He holds her.

GEORGE: The turtles. They'll be really happy.

INT. WILLIAM'S ROOM. MORNING

WILLIAM *hobbling about the room. He limps, curses. He massages his ribs, shoulders, arm. Curses.*

He suddenly stops, lifts his head, sniffs.

Sound from the cooker on landing.

WILLIAM *opens the door very quietly, peeps through the chink.*

SANDOR AT COOKER

SANDOR *shovels food from pan on to plate, goes to his room, shuts door.*

WILLIAM *goes on to the landing and stares at the cooker. It is filthy.*

WILLIAM *picks up cloth, holds it under tap, goes across landing, knocks at Sandor's door.*

SANDOR: Who is it?

WILLIAM: Me.

SANDOR *opens the door.* WILLIAM *holds up wet cloth.*

Clean the cooker.

SANDOR: I clean your cooker right enough. I break your bones.

WILLIAM *shoves the cloth into his face and knees him in the crutch.* SANDOR *doubles over.* WILLIAM *forces his head down and knees him in the face.*

SANDOR ON FLOOR, FACE BLOODY

WILLIAM'S FACE, UNCERTAIN

SANDOR'S FEET FLYING OUT

WILLIAM HITTING WALL

INT. WILLIAM'S ROOM
WILLIAM *lying on his bed.* MRS INCHCLIFF *sitting by him. He opens his eyes.*
WILLIAM: Where am I?
MRS INCHCLIFF: On your bed.
    Pause.
WILLIAM: Where's Sandor?
MRS INCHCLIFF: At the hospital. To get his nose done.
    Pause.
WILLIAM: How did I get here?
MRS INCHCLIFF: We carried you.
WILLIAM: Who?
MRS INCHCLIFF: Sandor and me.
    WILLIAM *looks at her.*
    A girl phoned.
WILLIAM: Oh? When?
MRS INCHCLIFF: About ten minutes ago. I said you were asleep.
WILLIAM: Well, I was, wasn't I?

INT. GEORGE'S FLAT. MORNING
The flat is on the top floor of a house in Hampstead. It is light, airy, silent.
GEORGE *and* NEAERA *are in bed. She is in his arms. He kisses her cheek, moves to get out of bed.*
NEAERA: Where are you going?
GEORGE: Coffee?
NEAERA: No. Stay.
    She kisses him.
    Stay. (*Pause.*) All right, you can go now.
    He moves.
    No. Stay. (*She snuggles into his chest.*) I'll make the coffee.
GEORGE: You don't want to make coffee.
NEAERA: No, I don't.

GEORGE: Well, listen. Will you just let me know when you're ready to order breakfast?
NEAERA: Yes. I'll let you know.
   They lie close.
   I'm ready to order.
GEORGE: What do you want?
   He takes her in his arms.

INT. WILLIAM'S ROOM. MORNING
WILLIAM *sitting up in bed in pyjamas, with coffee and toast.*
Footsteps. A knock at the door.
WILLIAM: Hello?
   HARRIET *comes in.*
HARRIET: I came to give you a lift. What's the matter?
WILLIAM: A slight chill. I think I'll stay where I am today.
HARRIET: Oh. Did you catch it on your day off?
WILLIAM: Possibly.
HARRIET: How was your day off?
WILLIAM: Oh, OK.
HARRIET: What did you do?
WILLIAM: I went to Cornwall.
HARRIET: *Cornwall?*
WILLIAM: Yes.
HARRIET: That's . . . a very long way, isn't it?
WILLIAM: It bloody is.
HARRIET: With that woman?
WILLIAM: That's right. She did well.
HARRIET: Did she?
WILLIAM: Yes. We put these turtles into the sea, you see.
HARRIET: You what?
WILLIAM: Turtles. We stole three turtles from the Zoo and took them to Cornwall and put them into the sea. That's why I needed the day off, in order to do that.
HARRIET: I don't understand.
WILLIAM: Why not?
   Pause.
HARRIET: I don't understand . . . what you're talking about.
WILLIAM: It's simple. That's what we arranged to do and that's what we did.

HARRIET: Turtles.
WILLIAM: Yes. (*Pause.*) Want a piece of toast?
HARRIET: Thank you.
  She sits on the bed.
  WILLIAM *gives her a piece of toast.*
WILLIAM: Here you are. They're on their way to Ascension
  Island now.
HARRIET: Who are?
WILLIAM: The turtles. Marmalade?
HARRIET: You're very chirpy this morning.
WILLIAM: (*Grinning*) Am I? Yes – I suppose I am.
  A sharp knock at the door. MRS INCHCLIFF *comes in without
  waiting for a response.*
  HARRIET *jumps up from the bed.* WILLIAM *stares.*
MRS INCHCLIFF: I think there's something wrong.
WILLIAM: Wrong?
MRS INCHCLIFF: Miss Neap. She won't answer the door.
  WILLIAM *gets out of bed.*
  I haven't seen her all morning.
  WILLIAM *goes to the door.*

LANDING
WILLIAM *and* MRS INCHCLIFF *go down the stairs to the floor
below.*

THE FLOOR BELOW
WILLIAM *and* MRS INCHCLIFF *approach Miss Neap's door.*

THE HALL
The front door of the house opens. SANDOR *comes in, a large plaster
over his nose. He stops, looks up the stairs.*

MISS NEAP'S DOOR
WILLIAM *knocks at Miss Neap's door. No reply. He tries the
handle.*
WILLIAM: It's open.
  In background HARRIET *appears on the stairs.*
  He opens the door.

159

INT. MISS NEAP'S ROOM
The room is dark, curtains drawn. WILLIAM *turns on the light.*
MISS NEAP *is sitting by a table in an armchair. One arm hangs over the side of the chair. Her head lolls. A large Snoopy dog is at her feet.*
MRS INCHCLIFF *and* WILLIAM *go to her.* WILLIAM *feels* MISS NEAP*'s pulse. On her lap, a* Book of Common Prayer *open at 'For the Burial of the Dead at Sea'.*
Behind her, on the table, an empty bottle of pills, a glass, a photograph of a girl of ten standing with her parents. An envelope propped up, addressed to Mrs Inchcliff.

THE LANDING AND STAIRS
HARRIET *looking down into Miss Neap's room.*
SANDOR *runs up the stairs, goes into the room.* WILLIAM *turns from* MISS NEAP, *murmurs something, looks up, sees* HARRIET, *comes out of the room, goes up the stairs to* HARRIET, *puts his arm around her, takes her up the stairs.*
MRS INCHCLIFF *comes out of the room, goes swiftly down to the telephone, starts to dial.*
SANDOR *remains, looking down at* MISS NEAP.
Over this, MRS INCHCLIFF*'s voice.*
MRS INCHCLIFF: (*Reading*) 'I have made all the arrangements for the cremation and have paid by cheque.'

INT. MRS INCHCLIFF'S KITCHEN
MRS INCHCLIFF, WILLIAM *and* SANDOR *at kitchen table. A bottle of whisky.* MRS INCHCLIFF *reading the letter aloud.*
MRS INCHCLIFF: 'I don't want a funeral service of any kind. I don't want anyone to be present. Please do not notify my mother until after the cremation. No flowers. Thank you. Flora Neap.'
MRS INCHCLIFF *puts the letter on the table.* SANDOR *pours her a drink.*
I never knew.
Pause.
WILLIAM: We never asked. (*Pause.*) She was just Miss Neap.
MRS INCHCLIFF: Do you think it's right – no service, no one there, no flowers?

WILLIAM: It's what she wanted.

SANDOR: Do it how she wanted.

Silence.

WILLIAM: (*To* SANDOR) How's your nose?

SANDOR: Nose no problem. But I am grotty a little. Minor
temperature. I have slightly vertigo, I stand up, room goes
round, floor is slanty. And you? How is your health?

WILLIAM: My floor's pretty slanty too.

SANDOR *raises his glass.*

SANDOR: I drink to Miss Neap.

They all raise their glasses, drink.

INT. NEAERA'S FLAT. EARLY EVENING

It has changed: brighter, crisper. Flowers. Bottles on the sideboard.
NEAERA *different. Her hair, her dress, etc. Her doorbell rings. She*
walks quickly to it and opens it. JOHNSON.

JOHNSON: Hello.

NEAERA: Oh, hello.

JOHNSON: Wondered if you'd like to pop in and have a drink?

NEAERA: A drink?

JOHNSON: We've been neighbours for years. But we've never
had a drink.

NEAERA: I'd love to. But I'm expecting someone in a minute.

JOHNSON: Ah. Another time, perhaps.

NEAERA: Mmnn.

JOHNSON: Snails behaving?

NEAERA: Busy cleaning up.

JOHNSON: Actually, they have tiny radio transmitters in them,
so I get to know everything that goes on in your flat.

NEAERA: Must make pretty dull listening.

JOHNSON: Well, I'll try again when I get back.

NEAERA: Where this time?

JOHNSON *smiles.*

JOHNSON: Oh . . . usual kind of thing. Bye.

He goes.
She turns to look at the snails in the tank.

EXT. ZOO. DAY

WILLIAM *walks towards the aquarium with a bottle of champagne.*

INT. AQUARIUM
WILLIAM *walks through the aquarium. He notes two baby turtles in the tank. He goes into the office.*

INT. OFFICE
GEORGE *and* NEAERA *sitting with sandwiches.*
GEORGE: Hello.
WILLIAM: Just passing by. Thought I'd drop this off.
NEAERA: Perfect. We're just having our lunch.
GEORGE: Couldn't be better.
  GEORGE *stands. Gets glasses.*
NEAERA: Like a sandwich?
WILLIAM: No, no.
GEORGE: (*To* WILLIAM) Oh, I told them, by the way. I told them I'd set them free. Left you two out of it. I said I was getting in a couple of babies and I'd set them free too, when the time comes.
WILLIAM: What did they say?
GEORGE: They made a few noises and then they shut up.
  He opens the bottle and pours. They drink.
WILLIAM: Good. Well, I have to go.
NEAERA: Do you?
WILLIAM: Yes, back to work.
NEAERA: I'll come out with you.
GEORGE: (*To* WILLIAM) Come back and see how the babies are getting on.
WILLIAM: I will.
NEAERA: (*To* GEORGE) Don't drink all the champagne.

INT. AQUARIUM
NEAERA *and* WILLIAM *walking through the aquarium.*
WILLIAM: Listen. What about doing it again – in about twenty years' time?
NEAERA: You mean when the babies are grown up?
WILLIAM: Yes.
NEAERA: Why not?
WILLIAM: I'll ring you nearer the time.
NEAERA: (*Smiling*) Right.

They stop. NEAERA *puts out her hand. He takes it. They look at each other.*
Well, cheerio then.
WILLIAM: Cheerio.
He opens the door. A shaft of brilliant sun. He goes out. She stands a moment. She turns, walks back towards the office.

EXT. ZOO
Long shot. WILLIAM *walking towards the exit.*

THE GIANT TURTLES, SWIMMING IN THE OCEAN

Victory

AUTHOR'S NOTE

I wrote *Victory* in 1982, working with the director, Richard Lester. The finance for the film was never found.

Harold Pinter

*A boat becalmed, far out to sea. The mast slowly sways. Heat haze.
Red sun.
Gulls encircle the boat, screeching.*

*Screeching violins. A ladies' orchestra. Bare arms. White dresses.
Crimson sashes.*

*A wall of foliage. Bamboo spears pierce the foliage, quiver, stay
pointed.
Camera pans up to see, through leaves, impassive native faces.*

*An island. Moonlight. Silence.
Figures of men seen from a distance at the door of a low, thatched
house. The door is kicked open. The sound reverberates in the night.
Explosion of shrieking birds.*

*Driving rain. Leashed, barking dogs leading men with rifles through
jungle.
One of the men suddenly turns in panic, raises gun to shoot.*

*Champagne cork popping.
Two men standing on a jetty. Champagne is poured into glasses.
In background a freighter leaving. Natives waving, cheering.
The freighter whistles.*

*A cylinder gramophone playing in a room. Rosalia Chalier singing.
Moonlight.
A girl's figure in a sarong passes, carrying a bowl of water.
In background a mosquito net canopy over bed. A man's body on the
bed.
The girl parts the netting, places the bowl on the bed, kneels on the
bed, looks down at the man.
The gramophone hissing.*

A creek. Night. Crackle of fire. Two figures seated in foreground.

167

Fire burning.
Beyond the fire two Venezuelan Indians poking long knives into fish.
They eat.
The two foreground figures remain still.
One of these raises a hand and wipes it on a silken handkerchief.

High up on a hillside two figures in the grass. Bright sunlight.
A girl's stifled scream.

EXT. SURABAYA HARBOUR. DAY
1900.
A large mail boat approaching the harbour.
The captain, DAVIDSON, *on the prow, looking towards the port.*
Small boats coming from the port. Boatmen shouting.

EXT. SURABAYA HARBOUR
The mail boat at anchor. From quayside DAVIDSON *seen in a sampan approaching the shore. Dozens of sampans and other small boats with painted wooden roofs and striped sails.*

EXT. QUAYSIDE
DAVIDSON *steps on to the quayside and hails a dogcart taxi.*
Hubbub.
On the quayside Malays, Chinese, Negroes, Arabs, Javanese, some Europeans. Native carriers with bamboo poles over their shoulders, baskets hanging front and back.
Stalls along the quayside: cloth, hardware, fruit, food-stalls, etc.

EXT. HOTEL GROUNDS. AFTERNOON
DAVIDSON *walking towards Schomberg's Hotel through the hushed garden.*
Another building glimpsed through the trees – the concert hall. Torn, fluttering bills stuck to tree trunks. DAVIDSON *stops to look at one of them:* 'CONCERTS EVERY NIGHT'.

EXT. HOTEL VERANDA
DAVIDSON *walks along the veranda. The screens are down. Silence.*
No one in sight.
He enters the hotel.

INT. HOTEL LOBBY
Empty. Blinds down. DAVIDSON *walks towards calico curtains and passes through.*

INT. HOTEL ROOM
DAVIDSON *stands in the darkened room. At the back of the room a shrouded billiard table.*
DAVIDSON *discerns, in the dim light, a form lying across two chairs. It suddenly sits up and stands.* SCHOMBERG.
SCHOMBERG: Yes? You desire?
DAVIDSON: Mr Schomberg?
  SCHOMBERG *pulls a bell.*
SCHOMBERG: What is it you desire?
DAVIDSON: Just got into port. Come to pick up Mr Heyst. We sail again at midnight.
SCHOMBERG: He's not here.
  A Chinese servant enters.
SCHOMBERG: Take the gentleman's order.
DAVIDSON: Nothing, thank you.
  The servant withdraws.
  I'd like to see Mr Heyst. He's expecting me.
SCHOMBERG: He's not here.
DAVIDSON: But I left him here – three weeks ago. He *has* been staying here?
SCHOMBERG: Yes.
  Pause.
DAVIDSON: Well, do you know where he is?
SCHOMBERG: He has left this hotel. (*Shouts*) Boy!
  SCHOMBERG *leaves the room.* DAVIDSON *stands still.*
  The servant enters, waits.
DAVIDSON: A citron, thank you.
  The servant goes.
  DAVIDSON *perches on the billiard table, looks about the room. Through calico curtains he sees* MRS SCHOMBERG *go into the lobby. She goes to a chair behind a raised counter and sits, without moving.*
  DAVIDSON *watches her and then goes through the curtain into the lobby.*

INT. HOTEL LOBBY

MRS SCHOMBERG *does not look at him.* DAVIDSON *examines a large poster on the wall:* 'CONCERTS EVERY NIGHT. LADIES' ORCHESTRA. ZANGIACOMO'S EASTERN TOUR. EIGHTEEN PERFORMERS'.

The servant comes in, gives DAVIDSON *his drink, goes.*

DAVIDSON: Is the orchestra still here?

MRS SCHOMBERG: No. They have gone.

DAVIDSON: Were they good?

> *Silence.*
> Italian, were they?

MRS SCHOMBERG: He's German. He calls himself Zangiacomo – for business. He dyes his hair and his beard black – for business.

DAVIDSON: Oh.

> *Pause.*

MRS SCHOMBERG: One of the girls was English.

DAVIDSON: Oh really? (*He drinks.*) Where did they go from here?

MRS SCHOMBERG: I don't know. She didn't go with them.

DAVIDSON: Oh? Why not?

MRS SCHOMBERG: She ran away.

DAVIDSON: (*Lightly*) Who with?

MRS SCHOMBERG: That friend of yours.

> DAVIDSON *stares at her.*

DAVIDSON: Eh?

MRS SCHOMBERG: Your friend.

DAVIDSON: My friend?

> *She is silent.*
> She ran away with Heyst? But that's . . . He could never do such a thing. It's . . . impossible. He's a gentleman.
> *She swiftly throws him a piece of paper, twisted.*

MRS SCHOMBERG: He left you a note.

> *He unfolds it and reads it.*
> (*Whispers*) I helped them. I tied her things in my shawl and threw them into the compound. I did it.
> *Through this, various growing sounds: footsteps and voices on the veranda. Pings of a bell.*
> Say nothing –

SCHOMBERG *comes in. He glares at them.*

SCHOMBERG: (*To* MRS SCHOMBERG) There are customers! What are you doing? Where are the boys? Do something!
 She slips from behind the counter and goes into an inner room.
 SCHOMBERG *and* DAVIDSON *look at each other.*

DAVIDSON: So you can't help me? You've no idea where my friend Heyst is?

SCHOMBERG: He's a pigdog. He's a criminal.

DAVIDSON: Has he run off with your cash box?

SCHOMBERG: He's run off with a whore.

DAVIDSON: Good Lord.

SCHOMBERG: A girl from the orchestra. This is a respectable hotel. Do you know what it cost me to build my concert hall? Seven hundred and thirty-four guilders. He's ruined the reputation of this hotel. It's an atrocity! He's a public danger. Everyone knows he killed Morrison. He was always a swindler, a ruffian, a spy, an imposter, a Schweinhund! I tell you – I will be revenged.

DAVIDSON: But where has he taken her?

SCHOMBERG: Where do you think? He's taken her to his island, where he thinks nobody can get at him.

EXT. HOTEL GARDEN. LATE AFTERNOON
DAVIDSON *leaving hotel garden. In background the concert hall. The garden still.*
Over this, sound of ladies' orchestra.

EXT. HOTEL GARDEN. NIGHT
Earlier.
The concert hall illuminated. The orchestra playing. Japanese lanterns in the trees.
Impression through screens: the orchestra in white muslin dresses and crimson sashes. Bare arms. Men drinking, smoking, etc. Violins. The music 'murdering silence'.

INT. HOTEL. HEYST'S BEDROOM. NIGHT
HEYST *lying on bed, awake, under mosquito net. Music rasping from garden.*

INT. HOTEL DINING-ROOM. DAY
HEYST *eating, alone.*
SCHOMBERG *telling story on the veranda. Loud laughter from the veranda.*

EXT. SURABAYA HARBOUR. DAY
HEYST *walking along the quayside. He passes a street market. The girls from the orchestra at various stalls, examining trinkets, etc.*
MRS ZANGIACOMO *ushers them along.*
HEYST *approaches a small house.*

INT. DOCTOR'S SURGERY. DAY
DOCTOR *examining* HEYST *with stethoscope. He completes the examination.*
DOCTOR: All correct, I would say. Shipshape.
HEYST: Ah.
DOCTOR: But you were right to come, however. Eighteen
    months is a long time. Never know what the body can get
    up to. No doctor on your island, Heyst?
HEYST: Nothing on my island. Some natives on the west coast.
    We have no social intercourse.
DOCTOR: Must be a funny life.
HEYST: It suits me.
    HEYST *begins to put on his shirt.*
DOCTOR: What happened to that partner of yours? Morrison.
HEYST: Dead. Died in Sussex. Went back to England. Died of a
    cold.
DOCTOR: Did he? Poor chap.

EXT. NIGARAGUAN CREEK
One year earlier.
PEDRO, *carrying bags,* RICARDO, *carrying cash box and* JONES *walking along beach to small boat. They climb into it.* PEDRO *picks up oars and begins to row. The boat moves away from the beach.*

EXT. HOTEL VERANDA. NIGHT
HEYST *lying on easy chair on veranda, eyes closed. Music screeching from concert hall. He opens his eyes abruptly. Stares at concert hall.*

Stands, walks across the garden towards it. Pushes calico curtain.
Goes in.

INT. HOTEL CONCERT HALL
Fiddles and a grand piano. 'An instrumental uproar'.
ZANGIACOMO *conducting.* MRS ZANGIACOMO *at the piano.*
Dutch and Eurasian businessmen drinking Jenever and beer.
HEYST *sits, grimacing.*
Music comes to an end. Applause.
The women come down from the platform and join men at the tables.
Some sit together at the empty tables, to be joined by men.
MRS ZANGIACOMO *and* LENA *remain on the platform.* LENA *is a*
slim, frail girl of nineteen. MRS ZANGIACOMO *arranging music at*
the piano. LENA *motionless.* MRS ZANGIACOMO *suddenly goes*
across to LENA, *bends over her, pinches her arm.* LENA *jumps up*
quickly and goes down into the hall, where she stands, uncertain.
MRS ZANGIACOMO *passes her roughly.*
Men and women moving about. LENA *remains standing.*
HEYST *gets up and goes to her.*
HEYST: Excuse me. That woman did something to you. She
    pinched you, didn't she? I saw it.
    She looks at him, speaks nervously.
LENA: And what are you going to do about it if she did?
HEYST: I don't know. What would you like me to do?
    Command me.
LENA: Command you?
    She studies him.
    Who are you?
HEYST: I am staying in this hotel – for a few days.
LENA: She pinched me because I didn't get down here quick
    enough.
HEYST: Well, as you are down here now, won't you sit down?
    They sit.
    Do you sing as well as play?
LENA: Never sang a note in my life. Never had any reason to.
    Pause.
HEYST: You are English?
LENA: What do you think?

HEYST: How do you come to be here, with this . . . orchestra?
LENA: Bad luck.

INT. HOTEL KITCHEN. NIGHT
Steaming saucepans, vats, etc. The ladies of the orchestra cooking for themselves.
SCHOMBERG *comes in, looks about, sees* LENA *in a corner of the kitchen stirring a saucepan, goes towards her. He touches her arm.*
LENA *throws his hand away from her. The other women observe this and turn away.*
SCHOMBERG: (*Whispering*) Listen to me. Listen. You're
    adorable, adorable. You're a thing –
LENA: Stop it!
SCHOMBERG: (*Whispering*) A thing of beauty. Put your trust in
    me. I'm in the prime of my life. Look at me. Listen. I'll
    sell this hotel, we'll buy another one, somewhere else, just
    you and me –
    She breaks away from him and leaves the kitchen.

INT. HOTEL. SCHOMBERGS' BEDROOM. NIGHT
MRS SCHOMBERG *sitting at dressing-table in her night clothes, looking into a mirror.*
SCHOMBERG *comes in. He stands, looking at her reflection in the mirror. She does not meet his gaze.*

INT. HOTEL. WOMEN'S BEDROOM. EVENING
Two ladies of the orchestra doing their hair. LENA *lying on her bed, crying into the pillow.*
The women speak in broken English.
FIRST WOMAN: Stop that crying, you stupid bitch!
LENA: I'm ill. Tell them I'm ill.
SECOND WOMAN: Cry-babies make me sick.
    FIRST WOMAN *leans over Lena.*
FIRST WOMAN: There's nothing special about you, my darling.
    MRS ZANGIACOMO *appears at the door. She claps her hands.
    The two women leave the room.*
    LENA *looks up.*
LENA: I'm not well.
    MRS ZANGIACOMO *goes to the bed, yanks* LENA *off the bed.*

LENA *falls to the floor, clutching the bedclothes.* MRS
ZANGIACOMO *pulls her to her feet.*

MRS ZANGIACOMO: If I have any more of this, we'll kick you
out and leave you in this place to rot.

INT. HOTEL CONCERT HALL. NIGHT

*It is the interval. Scene as before. The camera moves through men
and women drinking and laughing, to find* HEYST *and* LENA *at the
corner table.*

LENA: My dad was a musician. My mum ran away. He taught
me the violin. He was a drunk. He had a paralytic stroke.
They put him in a home for incurables. I had seven
shillings and sixpence in my purse when I left him in that
home.

She looks at him.

What country . . . do you come from?

HEYST: I am a Swede.

LENA: Oh. But what are you –

HEYST: I live on an island. I came ashore . . . on some business.
I'm returning shortly.

LENA: Oh, are you? Listen, what is the name of this place? This
town we're in?

HEYST: Surabaya.

LENA: You see, what happens is, we just come off a steamer, we
go to a hotel, we're locked up, we get on another steamer,
we go somewhere else, I never know where I am. And no
one cares if I make a hole in the water the next chance I get
or not. Who lives with you, on this island?

HEYST: No one. I like solitude.

Pause.

Have you thought of going to the British Consul?

LENA: What's that?

HEYST: He represents the British government. He might be able
to send you home.

LENA: There's no home to go to.

HEYST *looks at her.*

What did you mean by saying 'command me'?

HEYST: Precisely that.

They sit looking at each other.

The ZANGIACOMOs *go back to the platform, followed by the other girls.* LENA *stands and follows them.*

THE ORCHESTRA
LENA *playing the violin.*

EXT. HOTEL GARDEN. MIDNIGHT
HEYST *walking backwards and forwards under the black shadows of the trees. The Japanese lanterns are extinguished. They swing gently. He stops. He sees something white flitting between the trees. It disappears.*
Suddenly LENA *is in his arms, clinging to him.*
LENA: I saw you. I saw you. I had to come to you.
HEYST: (*Holding her*) Calm, calm.
    She becomes still in his arms.
    It will be all right.
LENA: I knew it would be all right the first time you spoke to me. You spotted something in me, didn't you? In my face. It isn't a bad face, is it? I'm not twenty yet. All these men – they pester me all the time –
    He takes his arms away.
    What is it? What's the matter? I don't lead them on. I don't look at them. Did I look at you? I did not. You began it.
HEYST: Yes. I began it.
    Pause.
LENA: I am dead tired.
    He holds her.
HEYST: I shall steal you . . . from here.
    Her body stills. She looks up at him.
    I shall take you with me. Will you come?
LENA: Yes. Yes.
    Pause.
    I will.
    Pause.
    Will you . . . take care of me?
HEYST: Yes.
    Pause.
LENA: What will I ever talk to you about?

HEYST: Your voice is enough. I am in love with it, whatever it
    says.
LENA: What is it called, your island?
HEYST: Samburan.

INT. HOTEL. HEYST'S BEDROOM. NIGHT
He goes into the room, stands, looks at his face in the mirror.

INT. HOTEL LOBBY. DAY
Long shot.
MRS SCHOMBERG *at counter.* LENA *standing by counter with a
newspaper.*
LENA *murmurs.*
SCHOMBERG *comes in.*
LENA *reads the newspaper.*
MRS SCHOMBERG *motionless.*
SCHOMBERG *passes through.*

EXT. SURABAYA HARBOUR. DAY
Long shot.
HEYST *talking to a Javanese boatman.*

EXT. HOTEL GARDEN. DAY
The ladies of the orchestra walking towards the concert hall.
HEYST *approaches, stops.*
LENA *looks at him, then away.*
The other ladies look at him.

INT. HOTEL BILLIARD ROOM. NIGHT
A clock ticking.
ZANGIACOMO *stands with* LENA. *She holds a lamp. He holds her
other hand. She watches him tensely. He strokes her hand.*
ZANGIACOMO: (*Softly*) You're a good girl. A good girl. Go to
    bed.
    She withdraws her hand.

INT. HOTEL LANDING. NIGHT
An unseen presence in foreground, breathing.

LENA, *with the lamp, appears at the bottom of the flight of stairs and climbs them.*
She reaches the top. A hand suddenly pulls her into an alcove.
SCHOMBERG: Ssh! No sound. I burn for you. I burn. You understand? Yes, you understand. That man, that Swede, is after you, isn't he? He talks to you. What does he talk about?
LENA: Nothing.
SCHOMBERG: He's a fool. Don't waste your time. He knows nothing of women. He's a hermit. He lives on a derelict island. He's a man of shadow. I am a man of substance. I know about women. God, your body.
He strokes her upper arm.
Your body. You will stay when the others go. I'll send my hag away. You provoke me, don't you? You deliberately provoke me.
He reaches for her breast. She breaks away. Her dress rips.

INT. HOTEL. SCHOMBERGS' BEDROOM. NIGHT
MRS SCHOMBERG *in bed. Sound of running footsteps.*
SCHOMBERG *comes in, looks at her. He undresses and gets into bed.*
SCHOMBERG: Put the light out.
She does so.

EXT. HOTEL GARDEN. NIGHT
Whispers. Shadows. A bundle thrown out of the window.

EXT. SURABAYA HARBOUR. DAWN
A boat sailing away.

INT. HOTEL DINING-ROOM. MORNING
The orchestra ladies, with MRS ZANGIACOMO, *at breakfast. They sit at one big table. One chair is empty.*
In background ZANGIACOMO *in the lobby.*
ZANGIACOMO: Schomberg! Schomberg!
SCHOMBERG: (*Voice over*) What are you shouting for? What is it?
ZANGIACOMO: What have you done with her?
SCHOMBERG: (*Voice over*) What, what?

178

He comes into the shot.

Who?

The ladies look at each other in foreground. One giggles. MRS
ZANGIACOMO *glares.*

ZANGIACOMO: Where is she? My youngest! My youngest child!
 She's nowhere. She's not in her room. She's nowhere.

SCHOMBERG: Who, for God's sake?

ZANGIACOMO: Lena, you fool!

SCHOMBERG: Lena?

ZANGIACOMO: Where is she? She has disappeared.

 SCHOMBERG *turns, goes out of shot, followed by*
 ZANGIACOMO.

INT. HOTEL STAIRS

SCHOMBERG *rushing up the stairs, followed by* ZANGIACOMO.

INT. LENA'S ROOM

SCHOMBERG *bursts in, followed by* ZANGIACOMO

Four beds. A violin sits on one bed.

ZANGIACOMO: I told you, she's disappeared, idiot! What have
 you done with her?

SCHOMBERG: Me? Nothing! Nothing! What –

 Chinese SERVANT *appears at the door.*

SCHOMBERG: (*To* SERVANT) What is it?

SERVANT: Mr Heyst has gone.

 He goes.

 SCHOMBERG *and* ZANGIACOMO *look at each other.*

SCHOMBERG: Heyst!

ZANGIACOMO: Heyst, Heyst. Yes. Yes, of course. This is your
 fault. It is your fault.

 SCHOMBERG *goes out, followed by* ZANGIACOMO.

EXT. HOTEL VERANDA

SCHOMBERG *comes along it with* ZANGIACOMO. *The ladies stand
in background. Chinese servants gathering in the garden.*

SCHOMBERG: (*Shouting*) Heyst! Ruffian!

 He turns to the ladies and the servants.

 When did he go? Who saw him? Did anybody see them?

ZANGIACOMO: It is your fault!

ZANGIACOMO *attacks him, hitting him in the stomach, going*
for his throat. They stagger into the garden, fall, roll over,
ZANGIACOMO *lunging wildly at* SCHOMBERG.

EXT. HOTEL GARDEN
SCHOMBERG *and* ZANGIACOMO *grappling on the grass. Ladies on*
the veranda. One screams. Servants climb up trees and sit watching.
SCHOMBERG *picks* ZANGIACOMO *up, throws him to the ground and*
falls on him. ZANGIACOMO *lies still, breath crushed.*

INT. HOTEL LOBBY
MRS SCHOMBERG *sitting at her counter, still.*

EXT. SAMBURAN ISLAND. DAY
LENA *and* HEYST *standing on the shore.*
Behind them a boat going away.

CHANG STANDS, LOOKING AT THEM

THE ISLAND — HER POINT OF VIEW
One long bungalow. Smaller bungalows across the clearing. Decay.
Trees encroaching on the bungalows. Jungle.

LENA'S FACE

EXT. SURABAYA HARBOUR. DAY
A mail boat at anchor.
Schomberg's launch among other hotel launches alongside it. Painted
on Schomberg's launch: 'SCHOMBERG'S HOTEL'. *Boatmen*
shouting: 'Imperial Hotel', 'Hotel Splendide', etc.

EXT. JONES'S FACE
He is leaning over the rail. He looks down at SCHOMBERG.
JONES: Mr Schomberg?
SCHOMBERG: At your service, sir.
JONES: I would like to take rooms at your hotel.
SCHOMBERG: Certainly, sir.
    JONES *withdraws.*

SCHOMBERG'S LAUNCH
JONES *and* RICARDO *climbing into the launch, followed by* PEDRO
with luggage.
JONES *has a long, thin face and a long, thin body. He wears a*
white suit.
RICARDO *is thick-set, muscular, pock-marked.*
PEDRO *is hairy, flat-nosed, squat and brown-skinned.*
JONES: (*Of* RICARDO) My friend must have the room next to
    mine.
SCHOMBERG: Certainly, sir.
    SCHOMBERG *looks at* PEDRO.
JONES: Pedro needs a mat to sleep on. Any grog-shop will do.
    SCHOMBERG *steers the launch towards the shore.* JONES *leans*
    back, closes his eyes.
    SCHOMBERG *catches* RICARDO's *gaze.* RICARDO *grins at*
    him.

EXT. QUAY
JONES *and* RICARDO *driving away in a carriage.*
SCHOMBERG *walking towards another carriage, followed by* PEDRO
with bags, very close behind him, muttering to himself in an
unknown language.
The carriage drives away.

EXT. HOTEL VERANDA. DAY
JONES *reclining.* RICARDO *sitting, shuffling a pack of cards.*

INT. HOTEL LOBBY
SCHOMBERG *comes in, looks at the two men on the veranda, collects*
the registration book, comes out to veranda.

EXT. HOTEL VERANDA
SCHOMBERG: I have found your man a place.
    They look at him.
    May I have your names, please? For my book.
JONES: Our names? Ah. Yes. My name is Jones. A gentleman –
    at large. This is Ricardo. Martin Ricardo. Secretary. Put us
    down as tourists.

EXT. SAMBURAN ISLAND. DAY

HEYST *and* LENA *standing.* CHANG *at a distance.*

HEYST: This is Chang. He's the whole establishment.

LENA: Oh.

    CHANG *impassive.*

HEYST: This is the house. The sun's too heavy to stand about.
You'd better go in.

    *He takes her to the steps of the bungalow. She leaves him,
crosses the veranda, goes in.*

    He turns back. CHANG *is pushing a truck along rusty rails. It
carries Heyst's bag and Lena's bundle. He stops the truck and
takes them out.*

    (*Pointing to bundle*) Put that in the bedroom. Bring another
bed from that small house – for me. I will sleep at the end
of the big room.

    CHANG *nods.*

INT. HEYST'S BUNGALOW. MAIN ROOM. DAY

LENA *is standing in the room. Shutters closed. Slices of light. She
looks about: a painting on the wall of a white-haired man sitting at
a desk, heavy furniture, dozens of books.*

CHANG *comes in with bundle. He goes into the bedroom, comes out,
goes out of the house.*

She goes into the bedroom.

INT. BEDROOM

*Bare. A large chest. Piles of books. Bed with mosquito netting.
She looks about.*

HEYST'*s voice.*

HEYST: (*Voice over*) Where are you?

LENA: I'm in here.

    He comes into the bedroom.

    I'm sorry. This is your room.

HEYST: No. Yours.

LENA: Mine?

HEYST: You have it.

LENA: No. No, no. I can't. I can't take your bed. I don't
want to.

HEYST: You're not taking it. I'm giving it to you.

LENA: But where will you –
　　HEYST *puts his finger to her mouth.*
HEYST: Not another word. Have you said good day to my
　　father?
LENA: (*Startled*) What?
　　He laughs.
HEYST: In here.

INT. HEYST'S BUNGALOW. MAIN ROOM. DAY
They come into the other room. He points to the painting.
HEYST: That's him.
LENA: Oh. He looks very gloomy.
HEYST: He was. And this is his furniture, and these are his
　　books. So when he died, you see, I brought him to live
　　with me here, at Samburan.
LENA: And now you've brought me.
　　Pause.
HEYST: Yes.
LENA: You've saved me.
　　Pause.
HEYST: There's only Chang – and me. It could become a prison
　　for you.
LENA: No.
　　*She suddenly sees cylinder gramophone and drops to her knees
　　to examine it.*
LENA: What's this?
HEYST: A gramophone. We can listen to music.
LENA: What music?
　　He looks at her gravely.
HEYST: Zangiacomo's Ladies' Orchestra.
　　She stares at him, and suddenly laughs.

CHANG STANDING IN THE CLEARING, LOOKING TOWARDS THE
HOUSE

EXT. HOTEL VERANDA. NIGHT
Men standing with drinks. RICARDO *walks on to the veranda.*
RICARDO: Any of you gentlemen care for a game of écarté?
MAN: Splendid idea.

SECOND MAN: Very good idea.

> RICARDO *turns, looks into the shadows.*

RICARDO: And you, sir, would you like to join us in a game?

> JONES *comes out of the shadows.*

JONES: What a good idea.

SCHOMBERG, HALF HIDDEN BEHIND LOBBY DOOR, LOOKING
OUT ON TO THE VERANDA

JONES *and* RICARDO *settling down to play cards with the two men.*

EXT. SAMBURAN. MORNING

HEYST *on veranda, looking towards the sea. He listens. Light
footsteps in the room behind him.*

LENA *comes out. He does not turn to her.*

HEYST: Where have you been?

LENA: I've been doing my hair.

HEYST: I was wondering when you would come out.

LENA: I wasn't very far. You could have called. And anyway I
wasn't so long . . . doing my hair.

HEYST: Too long for me, apparently.

> *Pause.*

LENA: Well, you were thinking of me, anyhow. I'm glad. Do
you know, it seems to me that if you were to stop thinking
of me I should not be in the world at all.

HEYST: What on earth do you mean?

LENA: What I said – just what I said. You understand what I
said.

HEYST: No, I don't.

LENA: I can only be what you think I am.

HEYST: Nonsense.

> *She puts her hand on his arm.*

LENA: Don't forget we're alone. There's no one else here to
think anything of me. Except Chang. And not even you
know what he thinks. Do you? And don't forget I don't
even know where we are, what this place is.

HEYST: (*Briskly*) There was a coal mine here. I was Number
One. The manager. A friend I once had – it was his idea to
start the mine. I agreed to help him. The business went
bankrupt. I stayed. Come.

He takes her hand.
Breakfast.
They go into the house.

INT. HEYST'S BUNGALOW. MAIN ROOM
Breakfast is laid on the table.
LENA: Is that why you were impatient for me to come? You
were hungry?
HEYST: Famished.
He picks up a small bell and rings it.

INT. HOTEL LOBBY. NIGHT
Suddenly the door kicked open. PEDRO *enters with tray, on which
are empty glasses.* SCHOMBERG *is sitting in the room, still.* PEDRO
puts tray down, waves his hand at it, mutters.
SCHOMBERG *pours drink into glasses.*
PEDRO *takes the tray, kicks door open, lurches out.*

EXT. HOTEL GARDEN. NIGHT
PEDRO *with tray going towards concert hall. He goes in through
curtains.*

INT. HOTEL CONCERT HALL
*A long trestle-table covered with a green cloth. Candlelight. Twenty
to thirty men around the table.* JONES *the banker.* RICARDO *the
croupier. Baccarat being played.* PEDRO *silently serves the drinks.*

INT. HOTEL LOBBY. NIGHT
MRS SCHOMBERG *on the stairway, looks into the darkened billiard
room.*
MRS SCHOMBERG: (*Whispering*) Come to bed.
SCHOMBERG: Shut up!
She goes.

EXT. HOTEL GARDEN. NIGHT
Shapes of men leaving the hotel grounds.
Candlelight going out in the concert hall.
JONES *and* RICARDO *walking towards the hotel.* RICARDO *giggling.*

INT. HOTEL BILLIARD ROOM
SCHOMBERG *in the shadows. Door into lobby ajar. A chink of light.*
The figures of RICARDO *and* JONES *pass through and go up the
stairs.*
SCHOMBERG *listens to the shutting of doors above.*
Silence.

INT. HOTEL. JONES'S BEDROOM. NIGHT
JONES *lying on bed, fully dressed, staring at the ceiling.*

INT. HOTEL. RICARDO'S ROOM
RICARDO *lying on bed, naked.*
The door opens, JONES *enters, closes door.*
RICARDO *does not move.*
JONES *goes to the window and looks out.*
Silence.

INT. HOTEL BILLIARD ROOM
SCHOMBERG *sitting in the shadows, licking his lips.*

EXT. SAMBURAN. DAY
CHANG, *in clearing, looking up.*

CHANG'S POINT OF VIEW: THE MOUNTAIN RIDGE
*Two white specks moving, high up on the mountain ridge. They
disappear.*

EXT. FOREST
HEYST *and* LENA *walking under enormous trees festooned with
creepers. Great splashes of light.*
They emerge on to the highest point on the island. Rocks.
She looks out to sea.

THE SEA AND HORIZON. HEAT HAZE

EXT. LENA AND HEYST
She shuts her eyes.
LENA: It makes my head swim.
HEYST: Too big?

LENA: Too lonely. All that water. All that light.

HEYST: Come into the shade.

They sit under a tree.

LENA: How could you . . . how could you live here alone?
Before I came. And you were coming back here, weren't
you? Alone. Before you found me.

HEYST: Oh, yes.

LENA: But why?

Pause.

HEYST: Temperament.

She looks at him, intently.

Well . . . Princess of Samburan . . . you're gazing at me.
What do you see?

LENA: You liked living here alone?

HEYST: Yes.

LENA: Then I don't understand why you . . . burdened yourself
. . . with me.

HEYST: You're not a burden.

Pause.

You were being persecuted. You were . . . cornered.

Pause.

Oddly, it was because of a cornered man that I found
myself here in the first place. He was in terrible debt. I was
able to help him. He was excessively grateful. He decided I
had saved his life, that I was his true, his only, friend. He
started the mine here. He implored me to become its
manager. It was absurd. I knew nothing about coal and I
suspected he didn't either. Anyway, I gave in. I ran the
mine, which naturally collapsed before the year was out.
And so that was the end of his dream.

LENA: What was his name?

HEYST: Morrison.

She starts, stares at him.

What is it?

LENA: What?

HEYST: What is it? You look –

LENA: Nothing. No, nothing. I – What name did you say?

HEYST: Name? Morrison. What of it?

LENA: He was your friend?

HEYST: Yes, yes.

LENA: Your partner?

HEYST: My partner, yes.

LENA: And he's dead?

HEYST: Yes, as I told you –

LENA: You never told me.

HEYST: Didn't I? I thought I had. But what is this? Have you heard the name before?

She sits still, biting her lip.

Did you ever know anybody of that name?

She shakes her head.

Well, what is this mystery?

LENA: I've heard the name. But I didn't know . . . that it was your partner he was talking about.

HEYST: Talking? Who?

LENA: He was talking of you. But I didn't know it.

HEYST: Who was talking of me?

LENA: In that hotel. That man, Schomberg, talking to my boss and – sometimes – to others. It was impossible not to hear what he said. He was so loud. He used to shout.

HEYST *laughs.*

HEYST: And what did he shout about?

Pause.

LENA: He used to talk of a Swede.

HEYST: He talked of a Swede? And what did he say of this Swede?

LENA: That he had had a partner called Morrison. That the Swede first got all he wanted out of him, tricked him, swindled him, then kicked him out to die – that he as good as murdered him.

He stares at her.

HEYST: And you believed it?

LENA: I didn't know who he was talking about. I remember him saying that everybody in these parts knew the story.

HEYST: Well, well.

Pause.

Can you remember any more? I've often heard of the moral

advantages of seeing yourself as others see you. Let us go
further. Can you recall anything else that everybody knows
– everybody but me?

LENA: Don't laugh!

HEYST: Laugh? I am not laughing, I assure you. The
abominable idiot!

He stands, walks away, stops.

Tell me – would you have gone with me if you had known
of whom he was speaking?

LENA: It was stupid of me to listen, stupid of me to remember
. . . and to repeat it to you.

HEYST: Schomberg! The man is an animal.

Pause.

Why should I care? I have never cared. It has never
mattered to me what anyone said or believed, from the
beginning of the world till the crack of doom. I have lived a
life of hard indifference. Do you understand? I have simply
been moving on, while others were going somewhere. No
aims, no attachments, no friends, no acts. I leave all that to
others. Let *them* live, as they call it. But abuse and kill
Morrison? No. He was an innocent. I respected his
innocence. I respected his dreams.

Pause.

LENA: You are not a murderer.

HEYST: But you believed it?

LENA: I didn't know you.

HEYST: But just now – when you heard the name – you were
moved – you were shocked –

LENA: Because of the name. That was all. Because of the name.

Pause.

HEYST: I feel disgust . . . at myself . . . as if I had fallen into a
filthy hole.

LENA: I can't believe anything bad of you.

*He stands, clenched, moves away violently, and then suddenly
swerves back, sits by her, takes her in his arms and kisses her.
She averts her face, lifts her arm against him.*

*He pulls her arm away. She resists. He seizes her roughly. Her
dress rips. He embraces her fiercely.*

EXT. HILLSIDE. DAY
Long shot.
Two figures descending. LENA *walks ahead of* HEYST, *apart from him.*
As they draw nearer we see that LENA *is in pain. Her dress is torn. She stumbles.* HEYST *is walking slowly. He stops. She continues, and then slowly stops. She stands for a moment with her back to him. He is still. She turns, looks at him. He walks to her.*
HEYST: (*Quietly*) Please . . . forgive me.

INT. HOTEL BILLIARD ROOM. AFTERNOON
RICARDO *sitting with pack of cards, shuffling. He looks up.*
RICARDO: Take one! Come on, man. Take one. Quick.
 SCHOMBERG *comes into the shot, takes a card from the pack.*
 Look at it.
 SCHOMBERG *does so.*
 King of Hearts. Right?
SCHOMBERG: Yes.
RICARDO: I can make you take any card I like nine times out of ten.
 SCHOMBERG *sits at the table.* RICARDO *shuffles the cards in a number of elaborate ways.*
SCHOMBERG: You're fond of cards?
RICARDO: Fond of cards? (*He laughs.*) Yes, you might say that. Picked it up at sea. Playing for tobacco. We'd keep a game going right through the night, round a chest, under a slush lamp. That was gambling for you!
SCHOMBERG: You were a sailor?
RICARDO: Bred to the sea from a boy. Worked up to be a mate. Then I met the guv'nor and I left the sea to follow him.
SCHOMBERG: Why?
RICARDO: Why?
 He stares at SCHOMBERG.
 Why should I tell you?
SCHOMBERG: You are by no means obliged to.
RICARDO: Because he spotted me, that's why. Like that! (*Clicks his fingers.*) He knew everything about me the moment he looked at me. And he . . . touched me inside somewhere.

(*He looks at* SCHOMBERG.) Waste of time telling you this,
really, isn't it? It's outside your grasp. Isn't it?

SCHOMBERG: What did he spot . . . in you?

RICARDO: Who I am. What I am.

Pause.

Sometimes I have a girl – you know – and I give her a nice
kiss and I say to myself: 'If you only knew who's kissing
you, my dear, you'd scream the place down.' Hah! Not
that I'd want to do her any harm. I just feel the power in
myself.

SCHOMBERG: I see.

RICARDO: Do you? Well, you and me, for instance, we're sitting
here having a friendly chat, and that's all right. You're not
in my way. But you don't mean a thing to me. You're no
more to me than that fly over there. I could squash you or
leave you alone. I don't care what I do. Or I might get
Pedro to break your neck. He'd catch you round the waist
and jerk your head backwards – snap! I saw him do it to a
big buck nigger once who was waving a razor about in front
of the guv'nor. He does it well. You hear a low crack,
that's all – and then the man drops down like a limp rag.

He smiles at SCHOMBERG.

Mind you, I wouldn't ask him to do it unless you irritated
me in some way. I'm a reasonable man.

SCHOMBERG: I know you to be a reasonable man. And I'm sure
Mr Jones is a reasonable man.

RICARDO: Mr Jones! He's no more Mr Jones than you are.
You're pig ignorant. He's a gentleman. I spotted it at once.
And he spotted me. Like that! And so I followed him. And
I've followed him ever since.

He bends down, touches his ankle.

Look. What am I doing?

SCHOMBERG: You're scratching your ankle.

RICARDO: No, I'm not.

RICARDO *straightens, with a knife in his hand.*

SCHOMBERG: Gott in Himmel!

RICARDO: Comes in handy. Suppose some little difference of
opinion crops up during a game. You drop a card. You
bend down to get it and you come up ready to strike. Or

you stay under the table. You wouldn't believe the damage
you can do under a table with a thing like this.

SCHOMBERG: I would.

RICARDO *slips the knife back into a sheath attached to his
shin.*

RICARDO: You know where I got this knife? From a savage in
Nicaragua. You know his brother.

SCHOMBERG: I . . . ?

RICARDO: Pedro. He was Pedro's brother. We'd run into a bit
of trouble, you see, the guv'nor and me. So we were hiding
up a creek in Nicaragua. We were carrying a cash box with
320 sovereigns in it and 500 Mexican dollars. The Mexican
dollars weren't much good in Nicaragua but we were
thinking of popping up to Mexico for a game of cards, you
see. Do you follow me?

SCHOMBERG: Oh yes. Yes.

RICARDO: Well, we came across this pair of alligator-hunters,
up this creek. So we shared their hut with them. It was all
right. Fresh fish, good game, everything lovely. No
trouble. And these certain people who were looking for us,
you see, they gave it up, as a bad job. But, unfortunately,
these savages smelt the cash box, you see. I saw them smell
it. And then I spied them sharpening their knives behind
some bushes. So I said to myself: 'Hullo. They mean
business.' Antonio was his name. The brother. The trouble
was we only had one revolver between us – the guv'nor's
six-shooter. Only five chambers loaded. No more
cartridges. Well, it was time for dinner. Broiled fish and
roast yams.

EXT. NICARAGUAN CREEK. EVENING

A fire. JONES, RICARDO, PEDRO, *and* ANTONIO *eating.* JONES *and*
RICARDO *silent.* PEDRO *and* ANTONIO *occasionally grunt to each
other. They cut their fish with large knives. They do not look up.*

RICARDO: How's the fish, guv'nor?

JONES: Terribly good.

JONES *finishes his fish.*

PEDRO *and* ANTONIO *are silent.*

JONES *wipes his fingers on a silk handkerchief. He sighs, puts*

*his hand behind his back, as if to get up, draws a revolver and
shoots* ANTONIO *in the chest.*
ANTONIO *pitches forward on to the fire.*
PEDRO *jumps up, runs away.* RICARDO *springs on to his back,
gets his hands round his neck, strangles him. They fall.*
RICARDO *continues squeezing.* PEDRO *is still.*
JONES *walks over and looks at him.*
He isn't dead.

RICARDO: Anyone else would have been dead. He's an ox.

JONES *remains looking down on* PEDRO, *gun in hand, while*
RICARDO *goes towards* ANTONIO'S *body.*
RICARDO *pulls the body away from the fire, picks up Antonio's
knife, drags* ANTONIO'S *body to a stream and kicks it in. The
body sizzles.*

EXT. THE CREEK. LATER
PEDRO *tied to a tree.*
The rope goes round his throat and trunk, a reef-knot under his ear.
RICARDO *asleep.*
JONES *sitting, smoking, by the fire, a blanket round his legs.*

EXT. THE CREEK. MORNING
PEDRO *tied to the tree. Eyes rolling, tongue hanging out.*
Along the beach JONES *and* RICARDO *setting up a mast on a small
boat.*
RICARDO *looks back at* PEDRO *croaking.*

RICARDO: I think he wants to say something, sir.

JONES: Oh, he's probably thirsty.

RICARDO: Shall I give him some water?

JONES: Well, if he's thirsty, he'll probably appreciate it.

RICARDO *collects a jug of water. He takes it to* PEDRO.
PEDRO *drinks. After drinking, he stares at* RICARDO.
JONES *approaches.*

RICARDO: He's asking to be finished off. As a favour.

JONES: Oh no, no. We'll take him with us. He could be useful.

RICARDO: But will he be manageable?

JONES: Oh, I think so. Cut him loose.

RICARDO *takes the knife from* ANTONIO'S *corpse. He
approaches* PEDRO. PEDRO *twitches, sweats.* RICARDO *goes*

behind him. PEDRO *wriggles. Suddenly becomes still.*
RICARDO *cuts him loose.*
PEDRO, *freed, feels his limbs. He looks up at* JONES. *He crawls towards* JONES, *puts his arms around* JONES*'s legs, embraces his legs.* JONES *withdraws his legs, gently.*
Right. Let's be off.

INT. HOTEL BILLIARD ROOM
SCHOMBERG *leans across the table to* RICARDO.
SCHOMBERG: Look here. Do you mean to say that all this really happened?
RICARDO: No. I was making it up as I went along, just to help you through the hottest part of the day. Bring me a glass of sirop. I'm parched.
SCHOMBERG *goes to the bar, takes a bottle of 'Sirop de Groseille' from a shelf, pours pink liquid into a tumbler, splashes soda-water into it.*
This is a dead-and-alive hole. Playing cards here is like playing cards in a nunnery. Bloodless. Dried-up nuns.
SCHOMBERG *brings the tumbler to him. He drinks.*
SCHOMBERG: I don't expect you're making a fortune out of them, either?
RICARDO: Peanuts.
SCHOMBERG: Then why do you stick here? Men like you – you need excitement – you need a challenge worthy of your mettle.
RICARDO: Yes, you're right. Challenge is the word. He needs a challenge. He gets these lazy moods sometimes. He's in one now. But give him a real challenge – and he'll tense up tight as a drum and go straight to the heart of the matter.
SCHOMBERG: (*Intensely*) Listen to me.
RICARDO *looks at him.*
Listen. I could put you on a track. On the track of a man.
RICARDO: Who? The man in the moon?
SCHOMBERG: No, no. Listen to me. I'm serious. This man lives on an island, alone. He's rich. He's a thief. He has plunder. He has plunder stowed away on this island.
RICARDO: How much plunder?

SCHOMBERG: A lot.

RICARDO: How do you know?

SCHOMBERG: I know.

RICARDO: What kind of plunder?

SCHOMBERG: Minted gold.

RICARDO: (*Muttering*) Minted gold, eh?

> *Pause.*

SCHOMBERG: And cash. I have cast-iron evidence of this.

RICARDO: Who is he?

SCHOMBERG: He's a Swede. A baron. A Swedish baron.

RICARDO: A baron, eh? These foreign titles are usually fake.
I'm a student of all that kind of thing, you see. Still . . . it
might interest the guv'nor. A fake baron. He likes a duel,
the guv'nor, especially if it's with a hypocrite. He doesn't
favour hypocrites.

SCHOMBERG: I'll give you everything. Directions, provisions, a
boat.

> RICARDO *stares vaguely over* SCHOMBERG's *shoulder.*

RICARDO: Oh yes?

SCHOMBERG: A fishing boat. A child could handle it. And at
this season the Java Sea is a pond. You wouldn't even get a
wet face.

RICARDO: Well . . . it might be of interest.

> SCHOMBERG *turns sharply and looks behind him.*

JONES LEANING AGAINST THE DOOR, LOOKING AT HIM

EXT. SAMBURAN VERANDA. NIGHT

Lanterns. HEYST *reading.* LENA *cutting pages of a book with a
kitchen knife.*

*In background in the room the cylinder gramophone playing. Rosalia
Chalier singing.*

She looks up at him.

LENA: I've done it. The book is ready to be read.

HEYST: Ah. Good.

> *He continues to read.*

LENA: What are you reading?

HEYST: Poems.

LENA: Read one to me.
　　Pause.
　　Will you?
HEYST: They're French.
LENA: You mean in the French language?
HEYST: Yes.
LENA: Oh. I wouldn't understand, would I?
HEYST: No.
　　Pause.
LENA: Unless you told me what it meant?
　　He slowly looks up.
HEYST: Why not read something yourself, in English?
　　Pause.
LENA: I'm sleepy.
　　She stands, goes to him, kisses him lightly on the cheek, goes into the house.
　　He remains reading for a moment, then closes the book, turns out the lantern.

INT. BEDROOM. NIGHT
LENA *lying in the bed.*
HEYST *comes in, looks down at her.*
HEYST: Are you asleep?
LENA: No. I'm not sleepy.
　　She reaches up, pulls him down. He sits on the bed. Her arms around his neck, she whispers.
　　Say something to me in French.
HEYST: Tu es très belle.
　　She looks into his eyes.
LENA: What does that mean?
　　He bends towards her. She flinches. He takes her face in his hands and kisses her gently.

INT. BEDROOM. NIGHT
Later. Moonlight.
Under mosquito net HEYST *lying on the bed.* LENA *sitting by him, bathing his naked chest and stomach with a sponge.*
He lies still, looking up at her.

EXT. JAVA SEA. DAY
*A boat far out to sea, becalmed. Heat. Three figures gradually
discerned reclining in the boat. The mast slowly sways.*

INT. MAIN ROOM. AFTERNOON
HEYST *standing in the open doorway, looking into a glass, trimming
his beard.*
LENA *comes into the room. She takes the scissors, begins to trim his
beard.*
HEYST: There is no need –
LENA: Why not?
    She trims his beard in silence and then gives him the mirror.
There. Am I a good barber?
    HEYST *laughs, uncertainly, takes the scissors, puts them in a
    drawer.*
    LENA *sits.*
You should try to love me.
HEYST: Try? But it seems to me –
    Pause.
What do you mean?
LENA: You should try to love me as people do love each other
    when it is to be for ever.
    Pause.
That is what I mean.
    HEYST *goes to her, looks down at her.*
HEYST: Nothing can break in on us here.
    *He bends, lifts her out of the chair. She throws her arms around
    his neck, clasping him. He holds her, swings her round. She
    kisses him, then looks swiftly over his shoulder, gasps.*

CHANG IN THE ROOM

THE ROOM
LENA *disengages herself and slips swiftly into the bedroom.*
HEYST *stares at* CHANG.
CHANG *does not move.*
HEYST: What do you want?
CHANG: Boat out there.
HEYST: Boat? Where?

CHANG: On reef. In trouble. White men.
> HEYST *stares at him.*
HEYST: White men?
> *In background* LENA *appears at the bedroom door and watches them through the curtain.*
> HEYST *leaves the room, followed by* CHANG.

EXT. CLEARING
Low sun, ruddy glare, long shadows from trees.
HEYST *running towards the jetty. He looks out to the reef.*

EXT. THE REEF
The boat ricocheting against the rocks on the ocean side of the reef. The water on the shore side of the reef is calm. Two figures glimpsed lying in the boat. Another figure crouched, stumbling.

HEYST AND CHANG IN CANOE
They row the canoe to the reef.
HEYST *climbs on to the reef, holding rope which is attached to the canoe. He attempts to control the rocking boat, slipping on the rocks. He finally manages to attach the rope to the boat.*
HEYST *jumps into the canoe and he and* CHANG, *with great effort, pull the boat round the reef into calm water.*
They tow the boat back towards the jetty.

EXT. THE JETTY
HEYST *and* CHANG *climb out of the canoe on to the jetty. They look down at the boat.*

EXT. THE BOAT
The boat rocking gently up and down by the jetty.
JONES, RICARDO *and* PEDRO *lying twisted in the boat. Their faces are blotched, blistered.*
RICARDO *tries to sit up, fails.*
A cork helmet floats alongside the boat. A large, earthenware jug, uncorked, rolls about.
RICARDO: (*Hoarsely*) Hello.
> *He suddenly stands, swaying.*
> Water.

HEYST *kicks a large brass tap projecting above the planks. It does not budge.*

HEYST: (*To* CHANG) Crowbar!

CHANG *runs to the end of the jetty.*

RICARDO *sits abruptly, choking.*

RICARDO: Water.

CHANG *runs back with crowbar.*

HEYST *levers the tap with a jerk. Water trickles out of the pipe and suddenly gushes.*

RICARDO *crawls to the pipe, squats under it, clutches the end of the pipe, gurgles as he drinks, water soaking him.*

PEDRO *sits up, charges, flings* RICARDO *away, sits under the pipe and drinks.*

RICARDO *picks up an oar and slams* PEDRO's *head with it.*

PEDRO *hangs on to the pipe.* RICARDO *hits him again.* PEDRO *lets go of the pipe.* RICARDO *kicks him in the ribs.* PEDRO *crawls away.*

RICARDO *looks back at* JONES, *who is still lying, supine. He helps* JONES *up, guides him to the pipe.*

Here you are, sir. Steady.

JONES *drinks.*

HEYST WATCHING

RICARDO AND JONES

RICARDO *looks up at* HEYST.

RICARDO: Forty hours. No water.

JONES *comes away from the pipe, tunic soaked. He steadies himself on* RICARDO's *shoulder, looks up at* HEYST *and smiles a ghastly smile.*

HEYST: (*To* RICARDO) Isn't that man of yours bleeding to death?

RICARDO: Man? He's not a man. He's an alligator. (*He shouts.*) Aren't you? Olé! Pedro! Dungheap! You're an alligator! Aren't you?

PEDRO: (*Weakly*) Señor?

RICARDO: (*To* HEYST) What did I tell you?

HEYST *signals to* CHANG *to stop the water.* CHANG *does so and stands still, crowbar in hand.*

JONES: I'm afraid we aren't presenting ourselves in a very
favourable light.

HEYST: Please come ashore.

JONES: Very kind.

Helped by RICARDO *from below and by* HEYST *from above,*
JONES *climbs on to the jetty.*

RICARDO *follows.*

RICARDO *bends down, scratches his leg, stays crouched for a*
moment, looking up at HEYST. *He then slowly stands upright.*

EXT. ISLAND

Long shot. Twilight.

PEDRO *climbs out of the boat with bags.*

HEYST, JONES *and* RICARDO *stand together.*

CHANG *and* PEDRO *stand on the periphery of the group.*

Silence.

THE GROUP

JONES: We are indebted to you.

He sways. RICARDO *helps him.*

RICARDO: Lost our bearings. Heading for Batavia. Lost our
bearings. Ran out of water. Sun beating down. Thought we
were dead.

HEYST: I am not able to offer you a share of my own quarters
but I can give you a temporary home. Come.

He moves away.

JONES *remains still.*

JONES: It is like a dream.

HEYST: Sir?

JONES: A jetty, a white man, houses – it's a dream.

Pause.

A lovely dream.

JONES, *swaying on* RICARDO's *shoulder, smiles at* HEYST.

LONG SHOT

The group walking towards a bungalow.

JONES: (*Voice over*) There is a settlement of white people here, I
take it?

HEYST: (*Voice over*) No, no. Abandoned. Abandoned. Long ago.
   I am alone.
   They walk up the steps of the bungalow.
   CHANG *tries to unlock the door. He puts his shoulder to it. It
   explodes in the silence, reverberating in the night.*
   They go in.

EXT. HEYST'S BUNGALOW: VERANDA. NIGHT
LENA *sitting in shadow. A lantern on the steps lights only her feet
and the hem of her dress.*
She watches HEYST *approach. Across the clearing a small fire is
now burning outside Jones's bungalow. Candlelight in the windows.*
HEYST *walks up the steps, stops.*
LENA: It's me.
   Pause.
HEYST: You can't be seen. Good.
LENA: Why?
   HEYST *does not answer.*
   Why good?
HEYST: I don't know.
LENA: Who are they?
HEYST: I don't know.

EXT. CLEARING. NIGHT
The two bungalows.
Moonlight. Stillness.

INT. THE BEDROOM. NIGHT
LENA *wakes up. She is alone. She gets up, goes to curtain, looks
through it into main room.* HEYST *opening drawers, looking into
them.*
She goes into the room.

INT. MAIN ROOM
A lantern is on low.
LENA: What are you looking for?
   He shuts the drawer.
HEYST: Did you see Chang in this room at all – last evening?
LENA: No.

HEYST: At any time?
LENA: No.
>   *Pause.*
>   What's the matter?
HEYST: I left you asleep. What woke you?
LENA: A dream. You've lost something. What is it?
HEYST: What dream?
LENA: You weren't by me. You had gone. I put my arms out. I
>   turned to you, but you weren't there.
HEYST: That's not a dream.
LENA: What have you lost? I have touched nothing.
>   *He turns to her.*
HEYST: Lena . . .
LENA: We are still strangers to each other. You don't know me
>   very well.
HEYST: I asked if you had seen Chang in here, last evening.
LENA: What has he stolen? Money?
HEYST: No, not money. There is no money.
LENA: What, then?
HEYST: Something . . . of a certain value.
LENA: Well, ask him to give it back to you.
HEYST: Mmnn.
>   *Pause.*
>   Go back to bed. I'll come. I'll just smoke a cheroot on the
>   veranda.
>   *He touches her arm.*
>   I'll come.

EXT. VERANDA. NIGHT
HEYST *walks on to the veranda, sits, lights cheroot.*

LONG SHOT
View of Heyst's veranda. Glow of the cheroot.
RICARDO *in foreground, watching.*
The cheroot is thrown into the night.

EXT. SAMBURAN ISLAND. DAWN
High shot.
Glistening. Birds.

INT. JONES'S AND RICARDO'S BEDROOM. EARLY MORNING
JONES *asleep.* RICARDO *dressed. He slips quietly out of the room.*

EXT. JONES'S BUNGALOW
RICARDO *comes out.*
PEDRO *on veranda, folding the boat's mast. He places two oars beside it.*
RICARDO *steps into the clearing.*

INT. HEYST'S BUNGALOW. MAIN ROOM
HEYST *comes out of bedroom, closes the door. He walks across the room, looks out towards the other bungalow.*

EXT. CLEARING
RICARDO *up a tree, looking down on the clearing.*
PEDRO *on the veranda.*
HEYST *appears, walking across the clearing to Jones's bungalow, knocks on the door, goes in.*
RICARDO'S *eyes follow* HEYST. *He then looks back at Heyst's bungalow.*
CHANG *suddenly standing by the side of the house. He disappears behind it.*
RICARDO *begins to descend the tree.*

INT. JONES'S BEDROOM
JONES *in bed. The door closing,* HEYST *inside the room.* JONES *sits up.*
HEYST: Good morning.
JONES: Good morning . . . to you.
HEYST: I hope you slept well.
JONES: Very well. Oh, terribly well. Thank you. Still quite
    weak, of course.
HEYST: Naturally.
JONES: We owe a great deal to you, Mr Heyst.
    Pause.
HEYST: How do you know my name?
JONES: You introduced yourself to us last night.
HEYST: I don't recall doing so.

JONES: Don't you? How strange. But I am right, aren't I? Your name is Heyst, is it not?

HEYST: And yours?

JONES: Oh, mine is Jones. And his is Pedro.

HEYST *turns to find* PEDRO *sitting in the corner of the room, by the door.*

INT. HEYST'S BUNGALOW. MAIN ROOM. MORNING

RICARDO *standing still in the room.*

Silence.

He looks about the room, at the bookshelves, the painting, etc.

His eyes go to the closed door. He goes towards it, slowly, and soundlessly opens it.

The curtain.

A faint rustle from within. He carefully moves the curtain and looks in.

LENA, *her back to him, combing her hair. Bare shoulders and arms.*

INT. JONES'S BEDROOM

HEYST: Where were you headed for – in your boat?

JONES: Madura.

Pause.

HEYST: Did you know I was living on this island?

JONES: You? I didn't know you existed, old boy.

Pause.

HEYST: Nevertheless, I believe there is something you want of me.

JONES: Oh?

HEYST: Yes. May I ask what it is?

JONES: Well . . . Mr Heyst . . . now that we have met . . . I mean now that I know you exist . . . there may be something I might want of you. But it's not urgent. I think I'll tell you what it is . . . the day after tomorrow – after I have given the matter a little more thought.

HEYST: What matter?

JONES: Oh, the matter . . . the matter . . . You and I have much more in common than you think, you know.

HEYST: I do not see that.

JONES: Well, we *are* both gentlemen, aren't we?

INT. HEYST'S BUNGALOW. BEDROOM
LENA *turns sharply.*
RICARDO *springs, puts his hand to her mouth. He holds her tightly with his other arm.*

INT. MAIN ROOM
CHANG. *He stands, listening.*
Scuffling, grunts, thuds, chair falling.
CHANG *leaves the room.*

INT. BEDROOM
LENA *knees* RICARDO *in the groin. He falls back, sits abruptly against the wall.*
He clutches his throat, squeezes his legs together. He stares at her.
She staggers, sits on the bed, adjusts her sarong around her, sits still, stares down at him.
A chair with a dress on it has overturned. Ricardo's slipper has come off.
RICARDO *looks at her with a half-smile.*
RICARDO: I wasn't going to hurt you. You surprised me, that's all.
> *Pause.*
> I didn't expect you, you see.
> *Pause.*
> Who are you? (*He massages his neck, grins.*) You're not tame, are you?
> *She remains still. He gazes at her.*
> You're a tiger.
> *Pause.*
> Listen, you wouldn't say anything . . . would you . . . to anyone . . . about this?
> *She slowly shakes her head.*
> Good girl.
LENA: What do you want?
RICARDO: Yes, you're a real tiger. Listen to me. I think we can be friends. What do you think? Do you think so yourself?
> *Pause.*
> You're my kind. Aren't you?
LENA: Am I?

RICARDO: Yes. I feel it. Here!

He punches himself in the stomach.

LENA: What do you want?

RICARDO: Money.

LENA: Whose money?

RICARDO: His money.

Pause.

Where does he keep it? Do you know?

LENA: What?

RICARDO: Does he keep it in the house?

LENA: No.

RICARDO: Sure?

LENA: Sure.

RICARDO: Where, then? Do you know?

She looks at him and then nods, slowly.

He takes her hand, clasps it.

You're my kind. Aren't you?

LENA: Yes.

RICARDO: Tell me something. Is he a good shot?

LENA: Yes.

RICARDO: So's my guv'nor. Better than good. I'm not so hot.
This is what I use.

He lifts his trouser leg. LENA *studies the knife strapped to his
shin.*

LENA: Aah.

Suddenly HEYST's *voice is heard.*

HEYST: (*Voice over*) Chang!

CHANG: (*Voice over, fainter*) Sir?

HEYST: (*Voice over*) Coffee ready?

CHANG: Sir.

RICARDO *turns to the door, reaches down, stays crouched, knife
in hand, facing the door.*

HEYST: (*Voice over*) Lena!

LENA: Yes, in a minute.

She touches RICARDO's *shoulder. He whips round to her, knife
at her breast.*

*She points to a window high in the wall, picks up a chair,
places it under the window. He moves to it.*

INT. MAIN ROOM
HEYST *looking out of the front window.* CHANG *comes in with a tray of coffee.*
HEYST *turns and looks towards the bedroom.*

INT. BEDROOM
RICARDO *gone. Shutters swinging at the window.*
LENA *sees his slipper. She picks it up, stands in the centre of the room, aims.*
HEYST: (*Voice over*) Lena! Breakfast!
LENA: Yes.
       She throws the slipper through the window.

EXT. BUNGALOW
RICARDO *under the window. The slipper flies through it. He catches it, puts it on. He whistles shortly.*

INT. BEDROOM
LENA *standing.* RICARDO's *whistle. She goes into the main room.*

INT. MAIN ROOM
HEYST *is sitting at the table.* LENA *comes in. He looks at her.*
HEYST: Your face is white. What is it?
LENA: No, nothing. I just felt a little giddy. I didn't want –
       She sways. He goes to her.
HEYST: You're ill.
LENA: I'll –
       Her eyes close.
       He picks her up, carries her into the bedroom.

INT. BEDROOM
He lays her on the bed, stands, closes shutters at the window. He sits with her. She clutches his hand, smiles, closes her eyes.

EXT. THE CLEARING
RICARDO *running along the verge of the clearing, keeping out of sight in the bush.*
He arrives eventually at the other bungalow. He stops, takes a deep breath, composes himself, goes in.

INT. JONES'S BUNGALOW. BEDROOM
JONES *sitting cross-legged against the wall.*
RICARDO *comes in.*
RICARDO: Ah! Sir!
JONES: Where have you been?
RICARDO: Oh, nosing around. Just nosing around. I knew you
    had company. I saw him come in.
JONES: You're out of breath. What's the matter?
RICARDO: Matter? Nothing. Thought I'd have a little run, that's
    all. Exercise.
    JONES *stares at him.*
JONES: Exercise?
RICARDO: So you had a talk with him?
JONES: You ought to have been here.
RICARDO: I will be next time. Just play him easy. We don't
    want him to start prancing. Play him easy. For at least a
    couple of days. I think I can find out a lot in a couple of
    days.
JONES: Oh yes? How?
RICARDO: By watching.
JONES: Why not pray a little, too?
RICARDO: (*Laughing*) That's a good one.
    Pause.
JONES: You can be certain of at least two days.
    Pause.
RICARDO: You trust me, don't you?
JONES: (*Slowly*) Trust you? Oh yes. I trust you.
RICARDO: We'll pull it off. Take my word.
JONES: Mmnn. I have a peculiar feeling about this. It's not like
    anything else . . . we've done. It's a different thing. It's a
    sort of test.

INT. HEYST'S BUNGALOW. BEDROOM
LENA *asleep.* HEYST *leaves her.*

INT. MAIN ROOM
HEYST *closes door to bedroom, softly. Turns.*
CHANG.
Silence.

CHANG: I go now.

HEYST: Oh?

CHANG: I no like this. I go.

    Pause.

HEYST: What don't you like?

CHANG: I know plenty.

HEYST: Oh do you?

    Pause.

    Are you frightened of the white men? Is that why you stole my revolver?

    CHANG *opens the front of his shirt, slaps his bare chest.*

CHANG: No revolver! Look!

HEYST: Well, where have you hidden it?

    He moves slightly towards CHANG. CHANG *jumps back.*

    If you give me back my revolver, no one will be frightened.

CHANG: No revolver.

    They stare at each other. CHANG *points to the bedroom.*

    I no like that.

HEYST: What?

CHANG: Two.

HEYST: Two? Two what?

CHANG: You no like that fashion, Number One, if suppose you know.

HEYST: What are you talking about?

CHANG: I go now.

    He goes.

INT. JONES'S BUNGALOW. BEDROOM

JONES *in same position.*

RICARDO *sitting.*

RICARDO: Mind you, I'll tell you the truth, sir, it's hard . . . to be patient. I find it hard. I want to rip him, you see. I want to rip him and have done with it.

JONES: But if you ripped him, old chap, you might never find your precious money.

RICARDO: *My* precious money? You're after the money as much as me, aren't you?

JONES: Oh, money isn't everything, you know.

    A knock at the door.

HEYST *comes in*.

Ah, Mr Heyst. Here you are again. Come in.

HEYST *closes the door*.

The door opens behind HEYST. PEDRO *comes in. He closes the door and stands by it.*

HEYST: I'm sorry to intrude.

JONES: Not at all, not at all.

HEYST: I have come to tell you that my servant has deserted – gone off.

JONES: Oh really? Why has he done that?

HEYST: I think he didn't like your looks.

JONES: Whose looks? Not Martin's, surely? I have always thought Martin was rather good-looking.

HEYST: All your looks. The point is that he is armed. He has a revolver. He doesn't like your presence here. I thought I should warn you.

JONES: But where has he gone?

HEYST: There's a native tribe on the other side of the island.

JONES: Oh, is there really?

Pause.

Rather a bore to lose a good servant. They're not easy to find. However, we have one (*To* RICARDO), haven't we? Why don't we let Mr Heyst have our Pedro?

HEYST: No. I couldn't possibly deprive you –

RICARDO: No, that's a good idea. Pedro can look after all hands.

JONES: He's a surprisingly subtle cook, actually. Aren't you, Pedro?

RICARDO: Damned good idea.

HEYST: It's really not necessary –

RICARDO: We'll send him over at once, to start cooking your dinner. I'll tell you what, I'll come and join you for dinner, in your bungalow, if I may? The guv'nor's still feeling weak, so I suggest we send his dinner over here, tonight.

He turns to PEDRO.

Like to cook special dinner for the gentleman tonight, Pedro?

PEDRO *stares at him*.

He's thrilled.

RICARDO *turns back to* HEYST.

Have you got the key to the store-room on you, Mr Heyst?
I'll give it to our Pedro.
Silence in the room. The three men stare at HEYST.
HEYST *slowly takes out the key, gives it to* RICARDO, *leaves the room.*
Silence.
I've got a little plan, sir.
JONES *says nothing.*
I think I'll shave.
He goes to his bag, takes out looking-glass, etc. Goes on to the veranda.
Pedro! Hot water!

EXT. VERANDA
RICARDO *takes off his shirt, hangs the glass, etc.*
JONES *watching him through the open door.*
PEDRO *brings a pan of hot water, puts it down.*
RICARDO *places the key carefully on the veranda rail. He begins to shave, humming.*
JONES *watches him through the open door.*

INT. HEYST'S BUNGALOW. BEDROOM. EARLY AFTERNOON
LENA *lying, eyes open.* HEYST *bending over her.*
LENA: I'm better.
HEYST: Can you walk?
LENA: Of course.
　　She sits up, swings her legs to the side of the bed.
　　I'm better. What is it?
HEYST: We must find Chang.
LENA: Find him? What –
HEYST: Come.

EXT. HEYST'S BUNGALOW
PEDRO, *in front of house, stooping over fire, with saucepans.*
HEYST *and* LENA *pass by him without looking at him.*
PEDRO *stands, stares after her.*
HEYST *and* LENA *go into the bush.*

211

EXT. JONES'S BUNGALOW. VERANDA
RICARDO *on the veranda. He gazes at the two figures going into the bush.*
PEDRO *running towards him.*
RICARDO *glances quickly inside the open door of the room, sees* JONES *sitting by the wall, eyes closed.*
RICARDO *walks quickly towards* PEDRO, *stops him.*
PEDRO: (*Pointing*) Woman!
RICARDO: (*Whispering*) Woman? Of course there's a woman. We know that. Now shut up! Go back! Cook dinner!
    PEDRO *goes back to the fire.*
    RICARDO *looks up towards the forest.*

EXT. THE FOOTHILLS
Two white figures disappearing.

EXT. THE FOREST
HEYST *and* LENA *approaching Chang's hut.*
HEYST *goes in.*

INT. CHANG'S HUT
Empty. Signs of hurried evacuation.
HEYST *leaves.*

EXT. THE FOREST
LENA *waiting.* HEYST *to her.*
HEYST: Gone. Let us go on.
LENA: Where has he gone?
HEYST: To the tribe.

INT. STORE-ROOM. AFTERNOON
RICARDO *ripping sacks. Flour, rice, dried fish, erupting from the sacks.* RICARDO *feverishly searching. Nothing. He stands still, sticks his knife into another sack, viciously rips it.*

EXT. HILL PATH
HEYST *and* LENA *climbing up precipitous path. At its top is a barricade of felled trees.*
HEYST: A barrier against the march of civilization.

They climb towards it.
They feared what was unknown, incomprehensible. And so
they built this barricade. It's understandable. I must say I
wish we were on the other side of it.
Lena seizes his arm, freezes.
LENA: Look!

EXT. BARRICADE
Through piles of freshly cut branches, spear blades protruding.

HEYST AND LENA
They stand still.
HEYST: Stay.
She holds on to him.
I won't approach near enough to be stabbed, I promise
you.
He moves forward.

EXT. THE BARRICADE
LENA's *point of view:*
HEYST *approaches the spears. He stops. Calls out in native language
for* CHANG.

EXT. THE BARRICADE
Spears pointing.
CHANG *suddenly appears through foliage, revolver in hand.*
The spears withdraw.

LENA WATCHING

HEYST AND CHANG
CHANG: Not come any close, Number One.
HEYST: What harm can we do you?
CHANG: Men come after. Bad for these people. I shoot if you
    come. Now – finish!
HEYST: All right. Finish for me. But let the girl come through.
    I implore you.
    CHANG *laughs.*
CHANG: She even more bad trouble.

HEYST: No, no. These men – they do not know she is on the
island.
CHANG: They know.
He points the gun.
They know.
The spears come back.

LENA *watches as the spears return.*
HEYST *turns slowly from the barricade, goes back to her.*
HEYST: He says no.
LENA: To what?
HEYST: He won't let you through.
LENA: Me? You were going to send me . . . in there? You
wanted me to leave you?
He is silent.
I would not have gone. I would not have left you.
She takes his hand.
He leads her to a view of the sea, looks down.
HEYST: I've thought of their boat. But they have taken
everything out of her. The oars and the mast. To put to sea
in an empty boat would be death.
She looks inland, starts.
What is it?
LENA: Something moving.
HEYST: No doubt we are being watched. What does it matter?
He sits, stares out to sea.

THE SUN BEGINNING TO SINK

LENA AND HEYST
LENA: Perhaps they are our punishment.
HEYST: Punishment?
LENA: The way we live . . . together. It is unlawful, isn't it?
He looks at her, laughs.
HEYST: You mean they are messengers of God? What God could
that be?
Pause.
Are you conscious of sin? I am not.

LENA: You took me up from pity. I threw myself at you. I am
guilty.
HEYST: (*With emphasis*) No. No. You are not guilty.
Pause.
Could I find the courage in me to cut their throats? The
problem is I have nothing but a pen-knife. But even if it
were a carving knife, would I have the courage? I've always
thought cutting throats a vulgar, stupid exercise.
Pause.
But to be totally without power – to protect you – that is a
bitter –
LENA: To protect me? It is you they are after.
HEYST: But why?
A gust of wind.
LENA: Look!

EXT. THE HEADLAND
'*Black on a purple sea. Great masses of cloud piled up and bathed
in a mist of blood. A crimson crack like an open wound zigzagged
between them, with a piece of dark red sun showing at the bottom.*'
HEYST: (*Indifferently*) A thunderstorm.

INT. JONES'S BUNGALOW. EVENING
JONES *standing. He wears a smoking jacket and a cravat.*
*He picks up a gun from a table and puts it in a drawer. He places a
chair.*
*He stands, uncertain. He goes to the drawer, takes the gun out, puts
it in the pocket of his jacket. The gun weighs down the pocket. He
takes it out. He rips his jacket off. He puts on a long, blue silk
dressing-gown. He puts the gun in the dressing-gown pocket.*
*He looks into a mirror and tears his cravat off. He stands,
trembling.*

INT. HEYST'S BUNGALOW. EVENING
PEDRO *laying the table. He goes out.*
Thunder.
After a moment, HEYST *and* LENA *enter.*
They stare at the table, laid for dinner.
HEYST *lights candelabra, takes it to the window, sets it on a table.*

HEYST: To let them know we're back. Let's finish the game.

LENA: There are three places laid.

HEYST: We have a guest. The shorter one of the two. He is like
. . . a jaguar. He is coming to dinner.

LENA sits in a chair.

Something is being worked out. Perhaps they don't know
what it is, either.

He picks up a table knife.

These are useless. Absolute rubbish – no edge, no point, no
weight. A fork would be better.

LENA: No. You need a knife.

A whistle from outside.

*HEYST walks to the window. Night has fallen. A flash of
lightning.*

HEYST: I have a crowbar somewhere. Could I stand in ambush
by this door? Smash the first head that appears, scatter . . .
blood and brains? And then do it again? And then do it
again?

LENA: No. It is a knife you need.

HEYST looks up at the painting of his father. He murmurs.

HEYST: He is responsible. The night he died I asked him for
guidance. He said, 'Look on. Make no sound.' That is
what I have done all my life. Until . . . you.

The door opens. RICARDO comes in.

Mr Ricardo, my dear.

RICARDO: At your service, ma'am.

He flings his hat into a chair.

At your service. (*To* HEYST) Don't like the look of the
weather. (*To* LENA) Pedro told me there was a lady about,
but I didn't know I should have the privilege of seeing you
tonight, ma'am. (*To* HEYST) Had a pleasant walk?

HEYST: Yes. And you?

RICARDO: Me? I haven't moved. Why do you ask?

HEYST: Oh, you might have wished to explore the island. But I
remind you it would not be totally safe.

RICARDO: Oh, that Chink. He's not much.

HEYST: He has a revolver.

RICARDO: So have you.

HEYST: Yes. But I'm not afraid of you.

RICARDO: Of me?

HEYST: Of all of you.

RICARDO: Oh. Aren't you?

> *The door bursts open.* PEDRO *comes in with a tray. He sets dishes of rice and fish on the table and goes.*
>
> Extraordinary strong brute, ma'am, that one. Not pretty though, I'd agree with that.
>
> HEYST *sits.* RICARDO *sits.*
>
> RICARDO *picks up a biscuit and eats it.*
>
> (*To* HEYST) Oh . . . before you start your dinner . . . sir . . . would you mind spending ten minutes with the guv'nor? He'd like to have a word with you.
>
> HEYST *looks at him.*
>
> He's not too well, and we've got to think of getting away from here.

HEYST: Getting away?

RICARDO: The best of friends must part. And, as long as they part friends, there's no harm done.

> *Pause.*
>
> Can I take you to him now? He's really keen to have a chat – before he can make up his mind to go away.
>
> HEYST *looks at* LENA.

LENA
She nods, almost imperceptibly.

INT. MAIN ROOM
They all sit quite still.

HEYST *stands abruptly.* RICARDO's *hand goes to his ankle, stops, scratches his leg.*

HEYST *goes to the door, looks out into the clearing. Lightning.*

RICARDO *takes* LENA's *hand.*

She looks at him.

HEYST *turns.* RICARDO *drops* LENA's *hand.*

LENA *stands, goes into the bedroom. The curtain falls behind her.*

HEYST: Your man is outside.

RICARDO: Yes?

HEYST: Get rid of him.

RICARDO: You want him out of the way?

HEYST: Yes. Get rid of him.

RICARDO: You mean you want him out of the way before you
let me take you to the guv'nor?

HEYST: That is right.

> RICARDO *puts his fingers to his mouth and emits a piercing*
> *whistle.*
>
> *A moment.*
>
> PEDRO *bursts in, looks wildly about.* RICARDO *raises his*
> *hand.* PEDRO *becomes still.*

RICARDO: Go to the boat. Now! Understand?

> PEDRO *stares.*
>
> The boat! At the jetty. Go there! You know what a boat is?

PEDRO: Si . . . boat.

RICARDO: Go to the boat. And stay there. Till I whistle.

> *He whistles shortly.*
>
> Till I whistle.
>
> PEDRO *goes.*
>
> The deal is on the square. God's honour. He'll stay there
> . . . till I whistle. Will you come along now, sir?

HEYST: In a minute.

> HEYST *goes into the bedroom.*

INT. BEDROOM

The bedroom is dark. HEYST *enters. A flash of lightning;* LENA
momentarily disclosed. He shuts the door, whispers.

HEYST: Lena.

LENA: Yes.

HEYST: You have a black dress. Put it on. Now.

> *Sounds of material sliding. He waits.*
>
> *She appears out of the dark.*

LENA: I have it on.

HEYST: You have a dark veil. Where is it?

LENA: I have it.

HEYST: Listen. I am going to see the other man. You
understand why?

LENA: Yes.

HEYST: Our friend is escorting me. As soon as we leave, go out
of the back door into the forest. Stay on the verge. Cover
your face with the veil, keep the house in sight. Wait in the

forest until you see three candles out of four blown out and then one relighted. When you see that – come back.

She takes his hand, gently, and holds it.

If you do not see that – before daylight – *do not come back.* You understand me?

LENA: Yes.

HEYST: In that case, go to Chang. Yes – to Chang. The worst he can do to you is shoot you, but he won't. I really think he won't, if I am not with you. You understand?

LENA: Yes.

She raises his hand to her lips and kisses it.

HEYST: Lena . . .

He kisses her, leaves the room.

LENA *alone.*

INT. MAIN ROOM

The bedroom door opens. HEYST *comes in.*

RICARDO *is standing by the desk. He turns to* HEYST *and smiles.*

EXT. THE CLEARING. NIGHT

Thunder. HEYST *and* RICARDO *walk towards Jones's bungalow. They go up the steps.* RICARDO *opens the door.*

RICARDO: Here he is, guv'nor.

INT. JONES'S BUNGALOW. BEDROOM

HEYST *and* RICARDO *come in.*

JONES *is standing, dressed in the blue silk dressing-gown, 'a painted pole'. His hands are in deep pockets.*

Two candles are burning.

HEYST *slowly walks into the room.*

RICARDO *stands, suddenly hesitant. He catches* JONES's *eye.*

RICARDO: I'll pop back. I'm on a track.

He leaves the room abruptly.

JONES, *startled, looks after him.*

HEYST *and* JONES *stand still.*

JONES: Awfully close, isn't it?

HEYST: I haven't come here to discuss the weather.

JONES: No, I suppose you haven't. (*Suddenly*) Don't put your hand in your pocket! Don't!

INT. HEYST'S BUNGALOW. MAIN ROOM
LENA *sitting in black dress, under candelabra.*
RICARDO *comes in.*
He looks at her, adoring. He moves towards her. She raises a hand.
He stops still.
RICARDO: I wouldn't harm you. You're my girl. You can feel
how quietly my heart beats. Ten times today when you,
you, swam in my eye, I thought it would burst out of my
ribs or leap out of my throat. It has knocked itself dead
tired, waiting for this evening. Feel how quiet it is.
Pause.
Speak to me.
LENA: What is your name?
RICARDO: Martin Ricardo. Martin Ricardo.
LENA: That's a very nice name.
RICARDO: Yes. It is. Thank you.
He draws closer to her.
Have you found out . . . where the plunder is?
LENA: Ah. Who knows where it is?
RICARDO: And who cares? You're right. You're my treasure.
You're my riches.
Pause.
Still, the money must be somewhere. We'll find it. No
trouble. Yes. But what you want is a man, don't you? A
master that will let you put the heel of your shoe on his
neck. Don't you? I live for myself – and you shall live for
yourself too. These 'gentlemen' make a convenience of
people like you and me. You see, we can both be free, you
and me together. You have found your man in me. Is that
your thought?
Pause.
LENA: Yes.
RICARDO: I'll rip him. I'll rip them both. Never in his life will
he go into that room of yours again – never any more!

INT. JONES'S BUNGALOW. BEDROOM
HEYST: I am not armed.
JONES: A question of prudence. That's all.
Pause.

I've heard of you, Mr Heyst.

HEYST: From whom?

JONES: We were staying at Schomberg's Hotel.

HEYST: Schom –

He stops.

JONES: What's the matter?

HEYST: Nothing. Nausea.

Pause.

Who are you?

JONES: Me? I'm just paying you a visit.

HEYST: For what purpose?

JONES: For your money.

JONES *brings a handkerchief from his left-hand pocket and wipes his face. He raises his right hand in his right-hand pocket.*

Don't move.

HEYST: I've told you, I am not armed.

JONES: You are armed. You are damn well armed!

Pause.

HEYST: What money?

JONES *studies him. He is shivering.*

JONES: I don't trust you at all, you know. I really think I should shoot you. Now.

HEYST: Yes. Do it. Why not?

JONES: Breeding. I suppose. Ha! But . . . don't misread me. I'm an adequate bandit.

HEYST: You're cracking an empty nut. There is no money.

JONES: Schomberg said there was! Martin told me there was!

He takes the revolver out of his pocket and cocks it.

Where did he go? Where is he? Why isn't he here with me? (*Violently*) He should be by my side!

He stills.

Money . . . money . . . one needs to play cards . . . to get the game going . . . that's all.

Pause.

My life – I'll confess it – has been a search for new impressions. I must say you've turned out to be something quite out of common. That's the truth.

HEYST: There is no money. Schomberg is mad. He persecuted

the girl. He was possessed . . . with an insane and odious
passion for her. What he has told you of money is to do
only with malice and spite. Don't you see that?
Pause.

JONES: Girl? What girl?
Pause.
Girl?

HEYST: Oh, Mr Jones, you can't expect me to believe that you
didn't know I was living with a girl on this island.
JONES *stares at him.*

INT. HEYST'S BUNGALOW. MAIN ROOM

RICARDO: With this.
He takes the knife out of its sheath.
LENA *takes the knife out of his hand, gently.*

LENA: Mmnn, yes.
She balances the knife in her hand.

RICARDO: It's been a good friend to me.
She holds it up to the light.
Listen, when we are going together about the world, you'll
always call me husband, won't you?

LENA: Of course.

INT. JONES'S BUNGALOW. BEDROOM

JONES *stands swaying against the wall.* HEYST *watches him.*

JONES: A girl? Well, well. (*He laughs.*) Yes, that's why he
shaved. He shaved under my nose. For the girl.

HEYST: No, he –

JONES: Yes! I smelt it then. I tell you what, old chap, he's let
me down. That's what it is. A gentleman is no match for
the common herd, or, at least, that is the view of the
common herd. Your . . . girl is of the common herd too,
isn't she, your creature? You could hardly have found her
in a drawing-room.
He giggles.
He shaved . . . right in front of me.
He points the gun.
Come.

HEYST: The girl is not there.
> *They go out.*

INT. HEYST'S BUNGALOW. MAIN ROOM
LENA *holding the knife.*
LENA: (*Softly*) I'll be anything you like. I'll do anything you
like.
> RICARDO *kneels, takes her foot, kisses it.*

EXT. THE CLEARING. NIGHT
Rain.
JONES *and* HEYST *approaching Heyst's bungalow. Jones's revolver
is at* HEYST's *back.*
Through the lighted door they see RICARDO *kneeling. He moves
from her foot to her leg up to her stomach. He remains, nuzzling her
stomach. She sits, throned, still, white.*
JONES *and* HEYST *stop.*
JONES: Ah. So the girl isn't there?

CLOSE-UP: HEYST LOOKING

JONES WHISPERING IN HEYST'S EAR
JONES: Look on. Make no sound. Mud souls, obscene. Mud
bodies. My . . . secretary. Look at it, kissing the belly of
the nymph, and then up through her body to her lips.

INT. HEYST'S BUNGALOW. MAIN ROOM
RICARDO's *head moves up to* LENA's *breasts.*
RICARDO: My love.
> LENA, *with the knife in her hand, looks down at him. She
> raises the knife.*
> *A shot.*
> *They fall apart.*
> RICARDO's *head is grazed. He falls away, staggers to his feet.*
> *Sound of running steps.* HEYST *comes in the door.*
(*To* LENA) Stick him!
He rushes out of the door.
HEYST *stands, looking down at* LENA.

She is bending over, her hands over her face. She leans back,
puts her hands to her breast. She looks up. Sees him.

LENA: Oh, my beloved.

Pause.

HEYST: Yes. He found you charming, the jaguar. Didn't he?
And it amused you . . . to charm him. Didn't it? It amused
you.

LENA: You mustn't make fun of me.

EXT. THE CLEARING

Rain.

RICARDO, *standing, holding his head.*

JONES *comes out of the shadows.*

RICARDO: Guv'nor! I thought he'd done for you. He nearly had
me just now.

JONES: No, it wasn't him. It was me.

RICARDO: Eh?

JONES: It's me now, too.

He shoots him.

RICARDO *falls.*

INT. MAIN ROOM

HEYST *has turned away from her.*

LENA: Don't make fun of me.

She droops in the chair, sways, half off the chair. He goes to
her, holds her.

The knife falls from her lap.

He tears her dress open.

A bruise of a bullet hole in her breast.

Her eyes open; looking down, she sees the knife on the floor.

Give me that. It's mine. I won it for you.

He gives her the knife.

What's the matter with me?

HEYST: (*Very quietly*) You have been shot.

LENA: Shot. Yes.

Pause.

Oh, my beloved. Take me in your arms, carry me out of
this.

*He lifts her in his arms, carries her to chaise-longue, gently lays
her down.
She looks up at him.*
Who else could have done this for you?
HEYST: No one.
   Her eyes close.

EXT. THE CLEARING
JONES *sitting on the ground.* RICARDO's *body lies close by.*
JONES *observing* HEYST *through the lighted windows, blankly.*

JONES'S POINT OF VIEW
HEYST *remains a moment, looking down at* LENA. *He then walks
into the bedroom. He looks down at the bed, picks up an oil lamp,
douses the bed with the oil, lights a match, sets fire to the bed.
He goes back into the main room, picks up another lamp, douses the
room, sets fire to it.*

EXT. SAMBURAN BAY. DAVIDSON'S BOAT. NIGHT
DAVIDSON *staring towards the island.*

EXT. THE ISLAND
The house in flames.

EXT. JONES SITTING, MOTIONLESS

EXT. THE JETTY. NIGHT
DAVIDSON *arriving in a small boat with two sailors. They jump out
of the boat, begin to run towards the house.
Out of the dark,* PEDRO *lurches towards them, jumps at* DAVIDSON,
seizes him. The two sailors pull him off, struggle with him.
DAVIDSON *runs towards the house.*
PEDRO *and sailors rolling on the ground·in the background.*

EXT. THE HOUSE. DAVIDSON'S POINT OF VIEW
The house ablaze. HEYST *sitting with* LENA *in his arms.*
DAVIDSON *rushes up the steps, is beaten back by the flames. He
turns, sees* JONES.
DAVIDSON: Help me, for God's sake!

225

JONES *puts his hand behind him, picks up his revolver, points it at* DAVIDSON. DAVIDSON *freezes.* JONES *drops the revolver, stares blankly at him.*

THE HOUSE
The figures of HEYST *and* LENA *no longer visible.*

EXT. THE ISLAND
Long shot.
The house, burning.
DAVIDSON *silhouetted at the window.*
JONES *still sitting, in the light of the flames, unmoving.*
Camera holds on the scene.